DE LOREAN

THE RISE, FALL, AND SECOND ACTS OF THE DELOREAN MOTOR COMPANY

MATT STONE

motorbooks

Quarto.com

© 2024 Quarto Publishing Group USA Inc.
Text © 2024 Matt Stone

First Published in 2024 by Motorbooks, an imprint of The Quarto Group,100 Cummings Center, Suite 265-D, Beverly, MA 01915, USA.T (978) 282-9590 F (978) 283-2742

Motorbooks titles are also available at discount for retail, wholesale, promotional, and bulk purchase. For details, contact the Special Sales Manager by email at specialsales@ quarto.com or by mail at The Quarto Group, Attn: Special Sales Manager, 100 Cummings Center, Suite 265-D, Beverly, MA 01915, USA.

28 27 26 25 24 1 2 3 4 5

ISBN: 978-0-7603-8471-8

Digital edition published in 2024
eISBN: 978-0-7603-8472-5

Library of Congress Cataloging-in-Publication Data available

Design and Page Layout: Justin Page
Cover Image: Justin Page
Photography: Matt Stone, unless otherwise noted

Printed in China

Our Thanks . . .

To begin, my biggest thanks to everyone at Motorbooks/Quarto Publishing that supported me in bringing this project from an idea in my head to the book you hold in your hands.

Additionally, to my friend, editorial client, mega car fool, and DeLorean owner and fan, Don Weberg, a guy with whom I share a questionable sense of humor, offbeat automotive tastes, and a love of automotive writing and photography. Thanks for your words, advice, and contribution involved in this project.

To *Il Mio Amico Speciale*, Franco Bay, PR guy extraordinaire, whom I've known and worked with for decades, now public relations chief at Italdesign in Turin.

To great photographers Evan Klein, Mel Stone Carlisle (yes, my daughter), and any others contained herein.

To James Espey, President of Classic DeLorean Motor Company (Classic DMC), who invited us into his business and shared anecdotes and materials related to DeLorean construction, maintenance, modification, and restoration. Additionally, to consummate DeLorean researcher and author Alexx Michael who made a bevy of archival photos available to us for use herein.

Great appreciation goes out to the Petersen Automotive Museum for its unending support and cooperation.

And finally, to you, Dear Reader. Thank you for reaching into your real or metaphorical wallet, PayPal, Venmo, Zelle, or piggy bank to buy and hopefully enjoy this book. If you had not done so, we'd have had no reason to publish it.

To my long-suffering wife, Linda, who helps with and supports everything I do, even when it means hours spent proofreading copy she may or may not enjoy or understand.

CONTENTS

To paraphrase the immortal Sir Winston Churchill, John Zachary DeLorean (JZD) was "a riddle, wrapped in a mystery, inside an enigma"—his comments originally made in 1939 describing Russia as a land that "plays by its own rules" (often confusingly and in contradictory terms). I never knew or met Mr. DeLorean, but I have studied him deeply, during tenures at Chrysler Institute of Technology, Packard, General Motors, and his own DeLorean Motor Cars, Ltd.

"JZD" has been alternately defined as "brilliant, crazy, arrogant, shy, caring, well spoken, narcissistic, selfless, inspired, foolish, polished, athletic, clumsy, honest, dishonest, instinctive, gentle, moody, frumpy, handsome, sexy, imposing, made-of-cardboard," and at least a hundred other descriptors that don't bear further repeating at, this early juncture. His story is unique in all the world.

Born of a hardscrabble Michigan upbringing and rising to mere steps away from the presidency of General Motors, he resigned from his lofty perch to form his own sports car company, putting his own name front and center. A risky move considering the security (financial and otherwise) afforded him by the 14th floor of the GM HQ. DeLorean is also legitimately and properly remembered as one of the fathers of the original Pontiac GTO muscle car in 1964. He always cut an imposing figure at 6'4", whether as the gangly high school basketball player, the buttoned down, gray-suited GM exec, the shaggy haired playboyish entrepreneur, or the somewhat maverick, individualistic car company chieftain—there was no missing John Z. DeLorean. He was married four times, twice to what we now refer to as Supermodels, and is the father of two children: a biological daughter with wife Christina Ferrare, plus an adopted son. During his single years, he dated actresses and more models—Big John was by any measure, a player.

He's all too often remembered, criticized, and labeled solely for his stainless steel, gullwing doored dream machine, his company's ultimate failure in a challenging automotive landscape, and for the unfortunate drug bust case

Opposite: So, DeLorean Motor Company (DMC) it is. For a time, at least one of the models or prototypes wore "JZD" on its nose, for John Z. DeLorean, which was the initial name of the umbrella corporation, but then DMC also became a part of the car's model name. *Evan Klein photo*

against him, no matter the fact that he was fully acquitted of all charges. For better or worse, it's the DeLorean car that's always remembered as a dazzling, unique grand touring sports car, and the time machine star of a trilogy of successful sci-fi nostalgia adventure films. Since the original DeLorean car production ended in the early 1980s, there have been numerous attempts by John DeLorean, and others, to resurrect the brand with a new line of cars. Yet the original stainless steel skinned DMC-12 continues to captivate, and his dream stays alive in the thousands of rabidly damning and adoring DeLorean owners, and many more non-owning fans and enthusiasts, who keep the DeLorean flames alight.

Several books have been written about DeLorean—man, company, and cars—but none recently, and none that look comprehensively at the entire story from a modern and unbiased viewpoint. Which is my goal here. This work isn't intended as a pure John DeLorean biography—as several of those exist, including his own highly enlightening autobiography. Yet not to include some of the building blocks of his complex persona would be to leave the structural concrete out of a building's foundation.

No matter, DeLorean—the man, company, and cars—offers a compelling story, if not several. As a journalist, book author, writer, photographer, and enthusiast, it is my goal to share much of that with you here. Please remember as we dive into the DeLorean story that not everything we talk about will be in pure chronological order because many activities were taking place concurrently—the ideation and design of the car, raising funds, building the factory and dealer network, assembling the staff and executive staff. A linear minute-by-minute recounting isn't the goal.

Enjoy the ride.

Matt Stone

John Zachary DeLorean was born January 6, 1925 in Detroit, Michigan, the eldest of four sons of Zachary and Kathryn (née Pribak) DeLorean. John's father, a mill worker, born Zaharia DeLorean, was Romanian, and his mother was of Hungarian descent. The DeLoreans lived a hardscrabble, lower middle-class life in suburban Detroit, father Zachary working at Ford Motor Company, active in union organization, while Mrs. DeLorean, besides being full-time mom to four strapping young sons, also worked at General Electric. John's father battled an inconsistent temper, alcohol, and possibly drugs, and his parents divorced in 1942.

By all accounts, John was a bright young man and applied himself as a student in school. He grew up fast and tall, reaching his full adult height of six feet four inches (1.9 m) by his senior year in high school. In his autobiography *DeLorean*, John recalled of his father: "Despite his drinking and our periodic separations, I also remember some good times with my father. He taught me to love working with my hands, a love that led, I believe, to my career in engineering." He was fortunate to attend Michigan's Cass Technical High, which in latter-day terms might have been categorized as a "school for gifted children." The school certainly fed his aptitude for engineering and technology. DeLorean did well enough at Cass Tech to earn a scholarship to Lawrence Technological University, a small Detroit college. Not surprisingly, Lawrence Tech, and other schools, were interested in the tall, lanky DeLorean as a basketball prospect. He got good enough at intramural basketball that he was asked to join and play for Lawrence's top fraternity. But the frat wouldn't accept his good friend Ben Fox because he was Jewish. Perhaps an indication of his later, lifelong commitment to ethnic, religious, racial, and workplace equality, DeLorean turned down the school and frat's offers to play basketball for them.

During his junior year in college, DeLorean was drafted. He would later admit that he didn't exactly get along with military life. He felt that the military likely viewed him as incorrigible. Conversely, he was disillusioned with the service, although he respected the need to serve and protect his country. In his autobiography, he wrote that "I think I went through basic training more times than any other soldier in history, which may make you pretty tough, but doesn't do much else for you."

Opposite: A teenaged John DeLorean certainly looks like the younger version of the GM exec he would become: dark hair, short and pinned down, large yet piercing eyes, heavy brows, and soft chin. It's a big evolution from here to the stong, scarred chin and mane of gray hair he became most identified with. *Wikimedia Commons photo*

After World War II, he was honorably discharged, and he returned to Detroit. His parents were by then irreparably separated. DeLorean went to work for the Public Lighting Commission as a draftsman primarily to help support a better family home life for his now single, although hard working, mother, and his brothers. He concurrently finished his degree at Lawerence Tech. For all of his intelligence and imposing physical presence, DeLorean admitted that he was inherently, if not cripplingly, shy. Rather than jump into an engineering job, he decided to try sales, in this case insurance. In his autobiography, he explained, "I was afraid to face people especially strangers," and that he was intimidated even by something so simple as wandering into a store to buy a pack of gum. "I knew if I was ever going to get ahead in life, I had to overcome these fears." Hence his brief tour of duty as a life insurance salesman. It was clearly not his thing: "Of all the jobs I had over the years, none was more difficult or unpleasant than selling insurance." Simply setting up sales appointments was abject terror for him. Perhaps potential customers sensed his earnestness and/or felt sorry for him because in spite of his personal challenges, DeLorean proved a good insurance sales agent. He won a number of sales prizes in the eight months he was in the business and brought home important and meaningful income to his family.

It was his uncle Earl, an employee at Chrysler Engineering, who suggested he go to the Chrysler Institute of Engineering. This allowed him an avenue into the automobile business, while still working part time to earn some income. All notions of poverty and insurance sales were thus vanquished,

Below: Even into the early 1950s, Packard was a prestigious marque known for building elegant high-quality cars, an ideal place for young John DeLorean to begin his automotive engineering career. Interestingly, the two cars on the right are Packards, and the third at far left of this photo is a Studebaker, the company with which Packard would merge in 1954. *Don Johnston_WVU/Alamy Stock photo*

Below: John DeLorean enjoyed his years at Pontiac, working with talented engineers and several excellent engineering-minded managers. He spent more than a decade of his career at Pontiac, finally as its GM Vice President and Divisional Manager prior to taking over Chevrolet. *David Crane/ Alamy Stock photo*

Packard was long known as an engineering powerhouse, yet its fortunes came to an end in 1962.

as DeLorean excelled at Chrysler. He graduated with a master's degree in engineering and a plethora of employment opportunities open to him, particularly and perhaps somewhat obviously at Chrysler, which was considered a leader in terms of automotive engineering at the time. He didn't want to automatically take the presumptive path at Chrysler and elected to shop his wares a bit. He knocked on Packard's Research and Development department's door, and it opened wide for him.

His first assignment at the financially troubled Packard Motor Car Company was the development of a new automatic transmission called Ultramatic, needed as an advancement over its first such transmission that was essentially a copy of the less than efficient Buick Dynaflow. DeLorean's imagination and creative juices were highly activated by this undertaking. He dove into the work, constantly contemplating and working at and through the technical needs and challenges required by this new powertrain component. Sadly, by the early 1950s, it was clear to everyone, inside and outside the company, that Packard's fortunes were waning and a lot of ship jumping was taking place.

John's boss at Packard, Forest McFarland, got a solid offer to take over the advanced engineering department at Buick and took it. This opened a senior spot at Packard, which DeLorean comfortably filled. At nearly the same point in time, he was tapped on the shoulder for a senior engineering manager's spot also at GM, in this case at Pontiac. He took the Pontiac job and ended up beneath the wing of Pete Estes, a legendary GM engineering manager who was moving to Pontiac from Oldsmobile. It was at Pontiac that DeLorean's independent streak began to surface. He recalled that "when I reached top-level management, there would come a time I believed that many of my ideas were more progressive than those of the men who were leading the company. When they didn't agree or wouldn't listen, I just ignored them. I would take actions that, when they succeeded, were not only good for the organization but would also figuratively tweak my co-workers noses a bit." Being generally a loyalist and team player, he felt this "sort of arrogance" was out of character for him, although often the result was positive.

John relished his work at Pontiac, toiling for strong leaders like Estes and Pontiac Motor Division Vice President Bunkie Knudson. A lot of his work resulted in meaningful innovative patents for Pontiac and thus GM. In his autobiography, DeLorean recalled, "For example: automatic car washes were becoming a big thing at the time, and they all had rather crude massive brushes that rolled over the hood, windshield, roof, and back of the car. All cars [at the time] in turn had bulky windshield wipers that stuck out and would routinely be torn off by the motorized car wash brushes. This led to great frustration for our car owners, until at Pontiac I created the recessed wiper concept. Today every upper line car uses concealed wipers." It was also at Pontiac that DeLorean got a front row seat to the notion that engaging styling plus vehicle performance sells cars, concepts he would often put to practice as his career unfolded.

"Under Bunkie Knudsen, the Pontiac division also began putting together top performing cars and entering stock-car and drag races," DeLorean wrote. "As a result, we won most of the major racing events over the next two or three years. We redesigned our existing car bodies, added high-performance engines, and suddenly had one of the hottest things going. We were no longer the 'little old ladies' division; we had the perfect cars for the growing youth market. Of course our profits rose substantially. Knudsen taught us all well, and he gets all the credit for showing us the direction."

DeLorean was soon recognized as a management leader on the move, and he rose steadily and quickly up the ranks of GM. He and several other managers at Pontiac recognized that "You can sell a young man's car to an old man, but you can't sell an old man's car to a young man." Riffing on these themes and Knudsen's penchant for racing, DeLorean and three other men brewed up an "optional equipment package" for the mid-sized Pontiac Tempest that effectively ignited the entire American muscle car phenom of the 1960s and early 1970s. This "super Tempest's" "*four*fathers" were John DeLorean (promoted to Pontiac's chief engineer in 1961), Pontiac engineer supreme Bill Collins, engine specialist Russ Gee, and Pontiac's outside marketing and advertising manager Jim Wangers. With this project, they divined, and defined, the seminal muscle car formula: put the largest, highest performing engine you had on hand into a lighter weight mid-size two-door platform; add your division's high-performance, "police pursuit" suspension and braking hardware; give it a

Above: Other than the exotic GT car that ultimately bore his name, the Pontiac GTO is the car John DeLorean is most strongly identified with. It was a straightforward engineering project and product development process to take the relatively lightweight, mid-sized Tempest, give it healthy big-block powertrain options, a better handling police pursuit suspension package, a jazzy name, and along with three other teammates, ignite the American muscle car flame in 1964. *GM Media Archive photo*

Above: Triple carburation was pretty exotic, hot roddy, or drag racey for an American production car in 1964, but the Pontiac 389's "3x2" intake system not only wowed onlookers when the hood was popped open, it also wowed most anyone else who dared to drag race against a so-equipped GTO. *GM Media Archive Photo.*
Below: The original Ferrari 250 GTO of the early 1960s was the quintessential production-based grand touring racing class machine—beautiful, fast, sturdy, and reliable. In its day, GTOs ultimately won every big international race they entered and several championships. Today, the best, most provenanced examples could run you $100 million.

burbly dual exhaust system and a catchy name; and a bread and butter mid-sized car becomes a youth oriented image and performance machine.

Pontiac's stout 389 cubic inch (cu in) (6.4 liters [L]) big-block V-8 was chosen over the division's 421 cu in (6.9 L) motor, as GM enforced a mandate at the time that engines over 400 cu in (6.6 L) were reserved for full-sized and luxury models—so the 389 (6.4 L) it was. Rated at a healthy 325 horsepower (hp) (239 kilowatts [kW]) and backed by a four-speed manual transmission or a two-speed automatic, it would certainly get the job done. Pontiac's "cop spec" suspension translated to firmer springs, shock absorbers, and anti-roll bars, meaning a car that could handle the newfound power. This $295 performance package included chromed air-filter housing and valve covers to dress up the engine bay, sparkling chrome dual exhaust pipe tips, and was only available in the two-door body configuration.

The team wanted a jazzy sounding, sporty European-inspired name for this special machine and found that inspiration in Italy from Ferrari. The latter built a thinly disguised race car called the 250 GTO, for *Gran Turismo Omologato*, intended to "type approve" or homologate (*omologato* in Italian) this race-bred machine for European *GT* production-based racing classes. Pontiac's GTO also earned several other lexiconic nicknames including "Get Turned On," "The Great One," and "Gas, Tires, and Oil." The ultimate performance Pontiac GTO model packed an optional engine, still a 389 cu in (6.4 L) but with "Tri-Power" induction in the form of three two-barrel carburetors on a special intake manifold, all raising the horsepower rating from 325 (239 kW)

to 348 (256 kW)—definitely Corvette territory. The whole notion was so compelling that *Car and Driver* magazine staged a "GTO vs. GTO" story metaphorically comparing the hot new Pontiac with the thoroughbred, race-winning Italian Stallion.

The "fourfathers" estimated they could sell about 5,000 Tempests equipped with the GTO performance option package. Instead, 32,450 customers opted for the hot new Pontiac. Wangers and the ad and marketing teams developed attractive, youth-minded advertising and promotions for the new car, and DeLorean, Gee, Collins, and Wangers became heroes in the halls of GM. The Tempest lineup was substantially restyled for 1965, and of course the GTO continued, while horsepower increased and handling further improved. It wasn't long before other GM divisions wanted aboard the GTO bandwagon, thus was born the Oldsmobile 4-4-2, the Buick Gran Sport, and Chevrolet's Chevelle Super Sport 396. The American muscle car was now truly a thing. The GTO became a full-fledged, standalone model (as opposed to a Tempest option package), and the rest, as they say, is history. It also became the stuff of racing and high-performance legend, selling strongly through the 1974 model year, ultimately making a return to the Pontiac lineup again for 2004–2006.

Instead of "four renegade Pontiac guys" working under the radar to develop performance-oriented models attractive to younger buyers, the product development teams began actively looking for those young buyers. DeLorean received glowing credit for Pontiac's success—conception, engineering, and

Left: The Pontiac Banshee concept coupe wasn't exactly a 7/8th scale '68 Corvette, but the look was so impossibly close that big GM dog Chevrolet barked loud enough to get the project shuttered long before it got anywhere near production— or the 'Vette's market share. But it did help create other program opportunities for Pontiac. *GM Media Archive photo.* **Above:** Not every American car enthusiast buyer knew exactly what GTO stood for or had ever seen a Ferrari GTO, but the initials looked good and sounded cool on the car and nobody seemed to care that it was clipped from an Italian grand touring sports and racing machine. *GM Media Archive photo.* **Opposite:** 1968 was really the GTO's halo year, with an all new and modern "coke bottle"–style body design, bigger engines, more performance, and *MotorTrend* magazine's Car of the Year award. *GM Media Archive photo*

In selling Pontiac's upper management on the innovative GTO high-performance equipment option, John DeLorean explained that "you can sell a young man's car to an old man, but not an old man's car to a young man."

marketing—and was rewarded with a 1965 promotion to head of the Pontiac division. At just 40, he became the youngest executive in GM history to earn his own division chief title. The product offensive took form on at least two fronts: the first was to jazz up Pontiac's sport/luxury oriented Grand Prix and the second was to develop a smaller, Pontiac version of a two-seater sports car akin to the Corvette. Several design studies and prototypes for this Corvette combatant were designed and built, running a variety of six-cylinder and V-8 engines. The concept car was called the Pontiac Banshee. The Banshee was very much DeLorean's baby, although Chevrolet—GM's proverbial "10,000-pound gorilla"—squashed this idea convincingly, rightly estimating that it would pirate sales and profits from GM's flagship two-seater Corvette, so the Banshee was all too quickly dead in the water. Yet, this handsome sportster did serve an ultimate purpose, which was to help Pontiac earn the rights to its own version of the Mustang- and Barracuda-fighting Chevrolet Camaro, ultimately named Firebird.

DeLorean and company rode the success wave throughout the mid-1960s, as the GTO continued to notch strong sales throughout 1966–1967, the new Firebird proved an instant hit for 1967, and the substantively remodeled GTO for 1968 earned *MotorTrend* magazine's prestigious Car of the Year award that year. The aforementioned Grand Prix earned a substantive redesign for 1969 and also proved a sales smash. The Horsepower Race was well and truly *on*.

DeLorean's success at Pontiac changed his daily life and career substantively. Previously, as chief engineer, product engineering was his primary focus. Now, as a division chief, he was ultimately responsible for production, planning, marketing, finance, sales, and dealership relations and issues—a much fuller plate. And it was at this level he got a deeper immersion in the sometimes muddy waters of American-style big-company politics. DeLorean didn't much like what he was seeing. By 1969, under his leadership, Pontiac had become an extremely popular GM division, and he was asked to saddle up GM's biggest horse, Chevrolet. A somewhat challenged Chevy was still the Big Kahuna in terms of market share, sales, and importantly, corporate profits. He became the youngest leader ever to assume the role of Chevrolet Division manager.

By his own admission, DeLorean had gained a reputation as a corporate maverick, not only for attacking the system from within but also his personal lifestyle. In 1985, he reflected that "I have been married three times [although he would make that four prior to his passing] but I have had only one mistress—my work. While in many ways I'm proud of this drive and devotion, I also recognize that it has contributed to personal failure in my relationships with others. This was particularly evident in my first two marriages. For me, each marriage was a deep and firm commitment I thought would last forever. Yet my life was always engineering. I could devote endless hours to the job, totally consumed by what I was doing, but I could never fully devote myself to another person. As a result, I never had a truly deep personal relationship with my wives. In fact, I never let anyone become the type of close friend and confidant I now know we all need."

John DeLorean married Elizabeth Higgins in 1954 when he was still a student engineer at Chrysler. As he neared 30, he noticed that many of his friends were already married and were having children, so he figured "why not?" The vivacious blonde was attractive and by all accounts fun and engaging, and it was a brief engagement before they married, and moved to upscale Gosse Pointe, Michigan, a long-time bastion of senior automotive industry execs. John admitted that "the insane drive that kept me at the factory seven days a week late into the night was grossly unfair to her. The ultimate failure of our marriage was entirely my fault." He also said she proved an ideal "executive wife", though they divorced in 1969.

Opposite: John with the second Mrs. DeLorean, Kelly Harmon. He clearly loved and appreciated her, while admitting that "they should have just dated," as they really had nothing in common on which to base a successful marriage. For one, she was less than half his age. This photo was taken during John's latter days with GM as he's still wearing his "GM executive haircut and color." *Bettmann/Getty Images.* **Right:** As a power couple, John and Cristina Ferrare simply gleamed; he the powerful automotive industry tycoon, and she the frequent "cover girl" model, author, and television host. *Robin Platzer/Getty Images*

John DeLorean dated actresses and other celebrity women, and married two of the world's top supermodels.

His description of his next marriage is also somewhat eye opening after admitting that he didn't seek out women who were independent or challenged him, due to his own insecurities: "One of the women who entered my life at that time [the late 1960s] was Kelly Harmon, the daughter of Tom Harmon, the famous University of Michigan football figure. Kelly was 20 [DeLorean was 44 at the time], a fashion model, and one of the most beautiful women I had ever seen." True enough, as Ms. Harmon was what we today refer to as a Supermodel and successful in fashion magazine spreads, print ads, and ultimately television commercials. "Kelly and I had no business becoming seriously involved. Not only was she more than 20 years younger than I was, but we had nothing in common. I should probably have simply had an enjoyable affair with her and then moved on to more mature relationships." DeLorean ultimately summarized this marriage, in 1969 immediately following his first divorce, as "a few months of wedded bliss, and then we realized we had made a mistake." She was anything but the typical "Detroit car executive wife", although she made an earnest effort to fit in with the other auto community "ladies who lunch". Unfortunately, she ended up more often being fodder for the Detroit wives' gossip network. DeLorean and Harmon divorced in 1972.

In between his marriages, it's no surprise DeLorean led a very active dating life—more models, actresses, and assorted female glitterati. Post Kelly Harmon, he didn't wait long to head straight back down the aisle. This time it was another big-game fashion model, Cristina Ferrare. The pair were introduced by stalwart GM dealership and racing team owner Roger Penske. Also, some 20 years DeLorean's junior, Ms. Ferrare was a highly successful model, actress, television personality, and book author. A statuesque smokey brunette with classic chiseled features, the new Mr. and Mrs. DeLorean made a striking couple. Cristina had been married briefly in 1969 followed by a hasty annulment and had no children. She and DeLorean married in 1973, and divorced in 1985, his longest marriage by far. They were together during the entire DeLorean Motor Company founding, ultimate failure, history, and subsequent drug trafficking trial.

John DeLorean married a fourth and final time in 2002 to Sally Baldwin, who survived him as his widow at the time of his passing in 2005.

And the Kids...

John's first wife Elizabeth was not able to bear children, second wife Kelly Harmon was pregnant one time, ending in a miscarriage. At the time of their divorce in 1972, DeLorean was suffering a variety of middle-age crises, feeling something was missing from his life, including a long-term happy marriage, and the privilege of fatherhood. A young woman patient of a doctor friend of his became pregnant by one of her college professors and planned to give up the child for adoption. DeLorean felt the strongest pull from this situation and elected to adopt this child; he certainly had the financial wherewithal to support a child as a single dad and could afford proper childcare and education. The child was a boy, born at the very tail end of John's marriage to Kelly; he named his son Zachary, which was his own middle name, in honor of his father Zaharia, Anglicized also as Zachary. When John married Cristina Ferrare, she officially adopted "Zach" when he was 14 months old.

John's first biological daughter, Kathryn, was born November 15, 1977, to John and Cristina. Kathryn has had a varied life and career and is most recently spearheading an attempted rebirth of the DeLorean marque and car, under the name of DNG (DeLorean Next Generation). ∎

Above: The seemingly perfect family was disrupted severely by the DeLorean Motor Company's financial failure, and also by John's drug-smuggling trial. Son Zachary was somewhat bitter over those circumstances and remains so today as an adult. Christina Ferrare DeLorean divorced John not long after the drug trial's conclusion, of which she attended nearly every in-court day. Daughter Kathryn "Kat" is at the forefront of one of the movements to reinvent the DeLorean brand and bring new DeLorean cars back into the marketplace.
Ron Galella/Getty Images

John DeLorean, his wife, and children gave the appearance of the perfect American family, yet much trouble lay ahead.

DeLorean's body and psyche began suffering the effects of middle age and the huge uphill challenges presented by assuming the leadership role of large, powerful, but struggling Chevrolet. Turbulent marriages, too many meetings, and too many cocktail parties and executive lunches fostered a considerable weight gain. He'd gone up several suit sizes, and his face became bloated and flushed. He looked in the mirror one day and said he was somewhat repulsed by what he saw. His doctor cautioned him that his physical condition, long hours, and mega high-stress job would come to haunt him healthwise. He took a month's vacation to rest, relax, and reassess his priorities. He decided to take the situation into his own hands and put himself on a strict diet and exercise program. He began losing weight (back down several suit sizes), feeling and looking better in short order. He also took other steps. At his barber's suggestion he adopted a slightly longer more youthful hairstyle (some called it "chunky feathering") and also dyed his hair back closer to its natural black, combating the gray that had begun creeping in (which later on he would ditch in favor of a very masculine, fashionable all gray look). He began dressing more stylishly, not always in the typical "GM 14th floor uniform" of a dark suit, white shirt, and dark tie. The transformation was remarkable—a new, younger looking, "more hep" John DeLorean emerged.

He also addressed a long-standing problem on his face, the result of a botched corrective jaw surgery when he was a youngster. A piece of his jawbone became impacted, so another surgery was required to correct that, yet the physical reconstruction job didn't go so well, although it did sharpen his somewhat jowly jawline and leave a raffish looking scar. He elected to leave it alone this time around, and combined with the weight loss and exercise regimens, he looked a somewhat "New John DeLorean."

Various writers and reporters at the time, and since, said that this was all a concerted effort to feed his personal vanity and make himself more appealing to the starlets and models he dated and married. DeLorean denied these accusations, confirming that his health revitalization actions were aimed at being a healthier, better, and longer living father to his new son. A decade later, John commented in his autobiography that "To this day, much has been written about this subject, but I don't recall anyone ever *asking me* about it directly."

Assuming the GM Divisional VP job at Chevrolet was a monumental undertaking. DeLorean commented in his autobiography that "Chevrolet was in a disastrous slide . . . having trouble in the marketplace, with customers, dealers, and of course profitability." John applied his engineer's principles of problem solving and took a deeply hands-on approach to properly fixing—not just patching—these challenges. He met with dealers, midline GM executives, design teams, factory workers, even customers, suppliers, and any constituency that could lend meaningful insight and advice on what the root problems really were and how to solve them.

It was at this point he began to address what he perceived as a systemic racism problem in terms of a lack of qualified (primarily) black dealer owners

YOU SHOULD HEAR WHAT THEY'RE SAYING ABOUT VEGA.

Left: Maybe, "you should not hear what people are saying" as much of it wasn't good with regards to Chevy's new small car line, the star-crossed Vega. Actually, early magazine reviews were positive, as the car looked good and performed reasonably well. The problems began when the engines began seizing and the bodywork rusted severely, then the commentary went south. *Archive PL/Alamy Stock photo*

and company execs. He "shook the tree" really hard attempting to balance the equation to the extent possible—even to the point of risking his career over these issues. To that end, he was accused of reverse discrimination against whites. He fought this with education programs and modernized, more egalitarian hiring and career advancement practices.

He rightly assessed that the influx of affordable, high-quality vehicles being imported from foreign countries (primarily Germany and Japan) would absolutely impact the American car market in huge ways. All of his research told him that Chevrolet, and in fact all GM, needed to improve engineering quality, including interior design fit, finish, and materials. Slowly, the ship began to right its course, and Chevrolet once again became the top brand in sales in America, with increased profitability for the corporation and its dealers, plus much improved used vehicle resale values—an important metric in the car business.

His success at Chevrolet, stacked upon his big wins at Pontiac, put him in the spotlight as future GM President. By nearly any measure, the compact Chevrolet Vega of 1971–1977 was an abject failure. Although handsome enough, it suffered more quality problems than one little car could seemingly hold. Under the internal code name Project 898, work began in earnest on this lineup of compact cars in 1969, and preparing and delivering the Vega entrees to customers fell squarely in DeLorean's lap. Its entire development cycle proved challenging at nearly every turn—the idea was to employ a Reynolds "sleeveless" aluminum block for the 2300cc inline-four engine family that would power all Vega models. The technology, while common today,

John DeLorean recognized many of the star-crossed Vega's problems upon his arrival at Chevrolet, but there wasn't enough time to properly address all of them.

> **"The entire Vega disaster reinforced all my frustrations with the [GM] system. I didn't have the political savvy to get the right things done; I didn't belong to anyone's clique. I was the perennial outsider, a radically different man from such survivors of the GM jungle as Ed Cole."**

wasn't yet ready for prime time. DeLorean's idea was to build the Vega as a high-quality, BMW–like lineup of premium, small Chevys, not just a cheap import fighter. There were body structure problems and initially a poorly designed cylinder head, which was reengineered just prior to production. The cars developed rust at the mere mention of rain. DeLorean initially referred to it as a "horrible little car." Even though many of the problems were cured over the Vega's seven-year production run, the reputational damage occurred early, and the car and DeLorean were somewhat star-crossed because of it.

Yet, before the Vega axe completed its downward swing, DeLorean was approached in late 1972 to take on yet another important challenge, that of group executive for the Car and Truck Group. This put him ostensibly in charge of Buick, Cadillac, Chevrolet, Oldsmobile, and Pontiac, plus the GMC Truck & Coach Division, and all Canadian car and truck operations. He of course became the youngest person ever to assume this role.

By this time, DeLorean was growing weary of GM's corporate political environment, and notions of his succeeding Ed Cole as GM president were waning. John said in his autobiography that "The entire Vega disaster reinforced all my frustrations with the [GM] system. I didn't have the political savvy to get the right things done; I didn't belong to anyone's clique. I was the perennial outsider, a radically different man from such survivors of the GM jungle as Ed Cole." He also said of the 14th floor "there was the occasional black, Hispanic, or woman around there, but I was the token weirdo."

On April 2, 1973, at the age of 48, John Z. DeLorean placed his resignation before GM Chairman of the Board, Richard Gerstenberg.

This of course raises the question of "did he jump or was he pushed?" Even though DeLorean had his supporters and detractors, despite the Vega debacle, he was viewed as a success maker and the proverbial "up and comer" in spite of his somewhat independent, often renegade ways and flamboyant personal life.

So, now a married father of two used to a very substantial income, on what had seemed a generally clear path to the presidency of GM, he found himself at the crossroads of "what should I do?" and "what do I do now?"

Along the way to a car and a car company of his own, DeLorean dabbled in other ventures: Grand Prix of America (much like the Malibu Grand Prix parks where miniature golf meets pint-sized open-wheeled race cars), Dahlinger Pontiac-Cadillac (car dealerships), DeLorean-Ryder Corporation (a commercial truck leasing concern, not unlike Penske Truck Leasing), Pine Creek Ranch (a real estate investment property), DeLorean Diesel Corp (a commercial engine company), and possibly others. In his book *GRAND DELUSIONS: The Cosmic Career of John De Lorean*, Hillel Levin summarized the ventures as "a relentless litany of failure" and went on to contend that "no one can ever make it big if they don't know when to spend. John fell on his ass as an entrepreneur because he refused to put money on the line. By the mid-seventies, every major enterprise DeLorean had undertaken was bankrupt, defunct, or defective." ■

2: BEG, BORROW, STEEL

Even resigning from GM at John DeLorean's level came with some options, choices, and a few strings attached. When you're as high up the corporate ladder as was DeLorean and making the kind of money he was earning, with a somewhat complicated and multilayered compensation package, there was more to it than simply dropping his resignation letter on the Chairman's desk and throwing the photos and paperweights from his desk into a box for transport home.

His income needs were by then considerable, as he and his family had acquired property and vacation homes on top of his Michigan residences. DeLorean explained it thus in his autobiography: "One problem with leaving GM was the way bonuses were paid. Each new position had given me substantial increases in earnings through bonuses. These bonuses, however, were paid over a five-year period, 20% a year. If I wanted to leave early, I either had to forfeit the bonus or resign to take a [GM] dealership that would allow me to earn out that bonus while no longer working in GM management. Historically a Cadillac dealership was a license to make a lot of money . . . When I was informed that a Cadillac dealership in Lighthouse Point, Florida would be mine if I wanted it, I suddenly had a way out," which would help him preserve his previously earned GM income.

"Instead of leaving GM and [immediately] becoming a car dealer, I made the transition by becoming the head of the National Alliance of Businessmen, an organization GM supported to the level of paying my salary but no bonus while I worked for that group. This would allow time for my dealership to be built and it was a nice move on the part of GM." This high-profile professional trade association was based in Washington, D.C., and made sense as a transitional move for DeLorean immediately post-GM executive ranks and whatever his next step would be, ostensibly a new Cadillac store in Florida.

"Unfortunately, my personal life was not as happy as my professional one. Cristina hated Washington, DC, and the intellectual society and social life there, where power politics determines who is invited where. She returned to Detroit with Zachary, and I ended up commuting on weekends, a situation I

Opposite: Back in the day, when someone left and/or was dismissed from the upper ranks of General Motors, it was common to offer them franchise opportunities to prevent them from going to work at rival car companies. John DeLorean was offered a Cadillac franchise in Florida, a worthwhile perk in those days as a successful Cadillac dealership in the right market could be very lucrative—JZD wanted car dealerships alright, but he wanted his cars on showroom floor and his name on the side of the building. *Patti McConville/Alamy Stock photo*

Three things you should know
before buying any fine car.

1. Total Cadillac value. That's everything you get in a Cadillac. Everything that makes it an American Standard for the World. Cadillac comfort. That superb Cadillac ride. It's all the features that come as standard on a Cadillac—features that often cost extra on other cars . . . if they're offered at all.

2. Cadillac resale value. It's consistently the highest of any U.S. luxury car make. Which means a Cadillac could cost less in the long run than you anticipated.

3. Cadillac repeat ownership. It consistently tops all U.S. luxury car makes. Cadillac owners tend to come back to Cadillac.

Haven't you promised yourself a Cadillac long enough? Whether you buy or lease, see your Cadillac dealer soon.

found tiring and frustrating." No matter, DeLorean's personal and career growth curve was about to spiral into stratospheres he could have never imagined.

"Finally, it [GM] was over. Although I had severed my connections with a company, I had served for 18 years, I was well-to-do, married to an attractive and vital woman, and young enough to pursue any business venture I desired." There was no question his talent, persona, and experience had value and were in demand, as he was constantly being pursued by a variety of businesses to either join their ranks in a top senior position or as board member. DeLorean could have lived a leisurely, high-paid lifestyle as a perennial board member and consultant.

Instead, he made another choice. "I decided to design and build my own car, to fulfill a dream I had been harboring for many years."

This is a dream that many have had throughout automotive history, some of whom acted upon it, while others never did. No matter, it's no easy undertaking—just ask Henry Ford (ultimately highly successful on an historic and global level, even after a few initial failed efforts), Preston Tucker, Gerald Wiegert (Vector Motors), the Studebaker brothers, Dr. Ferdinand Porsche, Enzo Ferrari, Messrs. Rolls and Royce, and countless others. Win or lose, it's hardly a cakewalk. This path is paved with varying degrees of rousing success, moderate success, abject failure, and personal disaster.

Setting Up Shop

John DeLorean had enough experience in the business to know that "it takes a village" and that he needed to form a company structure and assemble a team of talented people to design, develop, engineer, produce, market, sell, deliver, and service his dream machine.

It is interesting that DeLorean elected this time period in which to launch a new car company, as the transportation business, as a whole, was struggling in the early 1970s. It did, of course, make sense for his personal career trajectory, as he was ostensibly done with GM and had the time and energy to pursue a very personal dream. But the external challenges were myriad. One was the Organization of the Petroleum Exporting Countries (OPEC) oil embargo of 1973 and another was that carmakers were still learning how to successfully meet both consumer and legislative demand for increased vehicle safety measures and reduced vehicle emissions. The muscle car era that DeLorean helped foster in the mid to late 1960s was over (at least for the time being) and sexy hot, fuel-thirsty performance and exotic cars were decidedly out at that time. Vehicle performance and drivability for nearly every brand and in most vehicle segments were down, as carmakers grappled with making cars cleaner burning and more fuel efficient. Early 1970s technology supporting these needs and goals was in its infancy at the time. This was such a significant problem that certain exotic carmakers like Ferrari and Lamborghini had difficulty certifying their cars for import and sale in North America.

Opposite: After all of the umbrella companies, subcompanies, and potential model names, the original, now classic DeLorean model became the DMC-12. *Evan Klein photo*

The DMC badge on the car's grille stood for many things: DeLorean Motor Cars, DeLorean Motors Corporation, and ultimately the first three characters of the model name DMC-12.

Despite market realities, DeLorean formed the John Z. DeLorean Corporation, or JZD Inc., on January 1, 1974. Organizationally, JZD wasn't the entity that built the cars, instead lending its advice, consultation, business management, marketing, and production, and of course, DeLorean's name and influence. You might think of this as an umbrella corporation to the entities that developed, built, and sold the cars.

The next company structure step was a JZD, Inc., subsidiary company called Composite Technology Corporation (CTC), formed in October 1974, was intended as the arm of the corporation that would develop applications and production techniques for the Elastic Reservoir Molding (ERM) process for which DeLorean had taken a license from Royal Dutch Shell in the Netherlands. DeLorean was well aware of the challenges facing any car company, much less a new start-up, with reference to hampered performance and drivability and the need for increased safety and fuel economy, as noted above. His concept for an "ethical sports car" was already forming in his mind prior to a single line being drawn on paper. DeLorean knew that reduced vehicle weight and the use of high-tech construction materials and design were key factors in reducing fuel consumption, improving safety, and obtaining acceptable vehicle performance. Even though the use of advanced, lightweight composites is commonplace in today's vehicle production, and particularly in motorsport, it was advanced stuff in 1974. The ERM method of sandwiching structural foam between sheets of fiberglass was planned to be used in the DeLorean car. CTC was thus the first of a line of companies set up to develop, build, and sell DeLoreans.

Soon followed a litany of entities charged with various aspects of the project. It wasn't long before following the DeLorean corporate structure tree required a magnifying glass and a Geiger Counter. In October 1975, the

DeLorean Motor Company (DMC) was officially established, followed by the DeLorean Manufacturing Company. It has been alleged that this labyrinthine corporate structure with its divisions and subentities was constructed by John De-Lorean as a means to allow DeLorean and others to embezzle corporate funds, raised from private and government investment, for personal use and gain. There were also DeLorean Quality Assurance Centers, to which cars would be shipped prior to dealer delivery, intended to inspect, test, shake down, and repair any physical or mechanical issues before sale. Various other company footprints were set down in Irvine and Santa Ana, California, Bridgewater, New Jersey, and a decidedly executive, and upscale, corporate headquarters at 280 Park Avenue (at the corner of Madison Avenue) in New York. DeLorean felt that such a luxurious corporate space was necessary and beneficial as a successful public image for the company, while others inside and outside of the company felt it was a bit too lush and rich looking for a start-up.

Above: John DeLorean looked every bit the part of jet-setting car company exec, and his office digs needed to give the same vibe. Here he reviews a variety of car layout designs under consideration during early ideation days of the DMC-12's development; you'll note the consistency of mid/rear-engined platforms under review, such as the Fiat X1/9 and Porsche 914 (on the wall), and GM mid-engined prototype concept (model on table). *Arthur Schatz/Contributor/Getty Images photo*

John DeLorean very carefully curated his choice for his company's Manhattan HQ; he wanted it to appear impressive to customers, investors, dealers, and suppliers, but it was also a bit of a bargain at the same time, smartly subleased as fully built out space from Xerox.

John DeLorean had a ready and logical answer for those who criticized his new digs. The aforementioned space was master leased from the high-rise building's landlord by the Xerox Corporation. Needing to contract its business and expense footprint given the general economic issues of the time, Xerox had two half floor spaces that it vacated and could sublease out. The market price and demand for midtown Manhattan high-rise real estate had dropped by the time DMC was looking for its HQ. They were able to lease this expensively trimmed out space for less than market rates at the time and occupy it with relatively minimal upfit expense and purchased high-quality, barely used office furnishings and equipment for about twenty cents on the dollar. The location and visibility of this premium office space allowed DMC to appear a more successful and bigger fish than they were at the time. The 280 Park Avenue property was signed and known as the Bankers Trust Building, a good "storefront" allowing a certain immediate credibility. So, Park Avenue high-rise it was, two half floor spaces on the 43rd and 35th floor of the building at 280 on that famous Manhattan street.

Understanding the market competition at the time is important from today's viewpoint and of course critical to divining, designing, and producing the DeLorean car beginning in the mid-1970s. The most obvious and direct competition at the time was the Corvette. As a former GM employee, DeLorean was very familiar with this machine. It was at that time referred to as "America's only true sports car." In spite of emissions, safety, and fuel economy issues, the 'Vette still served up meaningfully competitive performance and legitimately had earned the status of an iconic American automobile and brand. Another bogie was the Porsche 911 and Carrera models. Porsche enjoyed a deserved reputation for solid engineering, performance, a sporty image, high build quality, desirable cache, and considerable motorsport success. DeLorean also mentioned Mercedes-Benz as a company with "great courage and leadership" in terms of engineering and producing premium products and also as an inspiration to equip his ethical sports car with exotic gullwing-style doors. In DMC's earliest days, Malcolm Bricklin's SV-1 was also a gullwing-doored sports car pitched as a "safety" car (the SV in its name stood for Safety Vehicle). Studebaker's avant-garde Avanti was thought of as appealing to the customer that DeLorean sought. It was a handsome, somewhat space-aged looking, comfortable automobile of advanced design with a performance flair and also wore fiberglass bodywork. Bricklin was ostensibly out of business by the end of 1975, but all the other models and brands previously mentioned were still in production and viable in the marketplace at the time.

Ever the engineer and product guy, DeLorean was focusing on the car he would build, and in early 1975 engaged the contract services of Giorgetto Giugiaro and his Italdesign transportation and industrial design firm of Turin, Italy (see Chapter 3).

The next major hurdles for the fledgling boutique carmaker was to raise mountains of capital to carry the company's already ongoing expenses (facilities, employees, consultations, and R&D) and to acquire and equip essential factory facilities. The original funding target was around $80 million, sourcing from John DeLorean personally, a limited partnership of investors, stock bought by dealers, a public stock offering, and a round of loans and bank funding. This amount proved to be not nearly enough and structurally isn't at all what ultimately took place.

Of course, there was also the question of where to establish a factory. In the meantime, early prototypes were under development during the latter portion of 1975 and into 1976. DeLorean and his managers cast about North America looking for suitable locales and acceptable subsidies and incentives to locate in one given area or another. DeLorean wasn't insistent that the car

Above: It should come as no surprise that the Corvette became among the DeLorean car's most obvious and best known bogies. It was considered America's "One True Sports Car" at the time and a car and brand that John DeLorean was most familiar with during his time at GM. It was also bodied in some material other than painted steel. Both cars in this serendipitous photo are 1981 models.

be made in the United States, although that was an early inclination. There were overtures and approaches from Detroit, Michigan (hey—why not the Motor City for America's newest motor car factory, along with United Auto Workers [UAW] to build it?), Alabama, Kansas, Texas, Pennsylvania, and also from foreign interests including Canada, France, Portugal, and Spain.

Plus, DeLorean received a particularly feature-laden overture from US territory Puerto Rico. This scenic island in the West Indies, a commonwealth of the United States, offered many logistical advantages in terms of air and sea shipping, plus was suffering an oppressively high unemployment rate at the time. The United States and local governments were highly incented to draw employment and economic stimulus to the island. The island was home to the now retired Ramsey Air Force Base, Strategic Air Command facility that was large enough to house the envisioned 500,000 square foot (46,452 square

Opposite, top: John DeLorean's impetus to employ gullwing-style doors on his car was primarily inspired by the original Mercedes-Benz 300 SL Gullwing coupe of the mid-1950s. There were some potential engineering benefits to this design, but realistically, most important to John were the cache and exotica factors this look added to the machine. **Opposite, bottom:** The Bricklin SV-1 also employed gullwing doors, although the company ostensibly was out of business by the time DeLorean's machine would be ready for the marketplace. *Vehicles/Almay Stock photo*

meters [m2]) factory facilities. The ever forward-thinking John DeLorean could visualize that the former base's massive runways accomplishing at least two important goals: allowing flights in and out for raw materials, supplies, and production components and also to allow completed cars to be air shipped out postproduction. It is purported that DeLorean had envisioned specially configured Boeing 747 jumbo jets carrying finished cars in the massive lower deck cargo area and also a passenger deck for visiting dignitaries, suppliers, dealers, and customers. And in addition to these aircraft uses, the long, flat, wide runways would serve as ideal test and evaluation tracks, something every carmaker needs near its factory.

In order to make the property pencil out for DMC's needs, it would have to be virtually given to the company gratis, plus loans and guarantees from the US and Puerto Rican governments to the tune of around $65 million. There was something to be gained by all sides. Puerto Rico's unemployment rate was hovering in the 30 percent range at the time, and the new DMC installation would put hundreds if not thousands of people to work, not to mention the financial spillover in terms of expenditures for fuel, utilities, food, hotel rooms, housing, and other economic boosters to the island. There was an important legal/logistical issue that required resolution prior to any such deal with DMC, which involved titling issues to the property that was supposed to have been claimed from various farmers via eminent domain and may or may not have been fully completed. Talks appeared to have been moving in the right direction (with reputed funding of up to $60 million from the two governments) when seeming "all of a sudden" in late 1977, another and far richer offer came in from Northern Ireland, for a massive industrial estate in Belfast. The deal was backed by Great Britain's Labor Party.

The Dunmurry, Belfast, property was large enough, and the money was right, yet this Irish territory presented legions of political, security, and economic challenges. Unemployment in this area was staggering at the time, with religious conflicts between Protestant and Catholic populations. There were ongoing riots, demonstrations, car bombings, kidnappings, murder rings, and all manner of civic and legal upheaval that racked the area and made the DeLorean factory prospect legitimately risky. However, local and Great Britain's governments made it clear that they intended to get these problems under control and that the prospect of so many jobs, attendant job training, and financial stability to the region would ensure that the DMC venture would be well received and safe.

Not to mention there was the matter of roughly $177 million in financial backing and concessions, about double what DeLorean originally felt was necessary to open his doors. The first bundle of money guaranteed to DeLorean was approximately $112 million, a combination of about $36 million in equity investment, $55 million in outright grants, and another $20 million in loans. With all other players seemingly out of the running at the moment,

Ireland—for all of its risks and potential—won the day and DMC was Belfast bound. The balance of the $177 million would come in the form of government loans and loan guarantees, plus whatever could be raised from dealers and private investors.

This piece of land in the "Dunmurry Industrial Estate" was as undeveloped as could be. It was summarily described as a "peat moss bog" and "field amid a war zone" but it was large enough to hold the projected factory and office buildings plus a road course–style test track. The British government and citizenry got something quite substantial out of the deal too, that being approximately 2,500 skilled jobs and the training of locals to do them—for some of these factory workers, a job at DeLorean would be their first real organized, paying career employment (outside of odd jobs, house painting, working at a store or bussing at a pub, and local handyman chores). In order to keep the religious balance of the factory floors on even keel, the managers hired equal number of Catholics and Protestants, and not just men—a substantial number of

Above: Porsche's seminal 911 was revealed in 1963, coming to market a model year later. It had evolved substantially by the early 1980s, offering the performance, build quality, reputation, and cache that DeLorean was after.

It is an odd juxtaposition that in the early 1980s, Porsche was seriously contemplating doing away with the 911's rear engine and air cooled architecture, just at the time DeLorean was developing a rear engined sports car.

women also populated the ranks, all supported by John DeLorean's long held principles of fairness and equality in hiring and employment equity beliefs.

Naturally, the locals were thrilled at these opportunities for people to work and support their families, all in the hopes that civil unrest would be substantially mitigated. Many non-Irish English weren't as excited about the deal, as they were picking up much of the tab for the entire venture at a time when other English businesses were allowed to fail, and yet the government opened a near $200 million dollar floodgate of money to what was essentially a foreign start-up company.

It was now up to the company's own "dog and pony road show" to get out and around and raise the final round of private finance in order to meet the requirements of the major funding agreement. The program was aimed at heavy hitter investors who had the wherewithal, and hopefully the interest, of investing at least $500,000. The goal from this tour of duty was to net approximately $15 million, after fees to Oppenheimer & Company, which was hosting and managing the financial instruments.

These gatherings most often took place in hotels and other ballrooms and were elegant, catered affairs attended by John DeLorean and many members of his senior staff, plus already committed investors and dealers. Perhaps given his inherently shy nature or just the business of asking for money (something not directly on his plate at GM), John generally disliked these events. He knew it was "part of the deal" and that he had to work this process in order to fully get the company, his factory, and car production off the ground. He did it generally with aplomb, able to turn on the charm and schmooze when he needed to, although it was made easier by the fact that he was talking to people and pitching something so deeply close to his heart and ultimate career dream. The investment instruments were structured primarily as research and development programs, offering meaningful tax benefits should the project fail and considerable earnings upside should the company and cars be a profitable success.

The "King of Late-Night TV" Johnny Carson was famously one of these investors, reputedly putting the requisite half million dollars into the program. His investment, given his considerable name value as a DeLorean insider, included his very own DeLorean automobile. Naturally, a plethora of publicity photos of "John and Johnny" were released to the media hoping to riff of this popular entertainment figure's involvement.

The moral is they got it done, and DeLorean (both man and company) had primary funding and a free plot of land, so it was time to truly design, develop, and production engineer the car; secure the necessary supplier relationships; and build out and fit the Belfast factory and assembly lines. ∎

∃: THE STAINLESS STEEL DREAM

t is logical that John DeLorean, being primarily an engineer and car guy, not passionately a finance or organizational guy, began forming ideas in his head about what the new car bearing his name should be like and all about. He logically reasoned that producing high volume mainstream machines that would compete with bread-and-butter models from GM, Ford, Chrysler, and American Motors is beyond the reach of a small start-up company, but that low volume, niche sports cars was a logical and attainable goal. So, a DeLorean sports car it would be. Safety was also a prime driver for John DeLorean. He contemplated the use of airbags before they became so prevalent within a decade of the genesis of his company and car. He also envisioned other passive safety measures such as padded steering wheels and a padded lower dashboard area.

He also wanted to minimize the "planned obsolescence" that was seemingly baked into the makeup of so many cars on the road: inadequate design, cars that rotted and rusted, fuel tanks that rotted through and leaked gas, powertrains that didn't go long miles, and cars that looked old only a year or two after being produced. He had early on decided that his car would be built around a mid- and rear-engine configuration. By this point, most of the top models from the premium Italian exotic carmakers were also mid- and rear-engined examples: witness the Porsche 911 and Carrera (decidedly rear-engine), the Ferrari Berlinetta Boxer, Lamborghini's Countach and Urraco, and Maserati's Bora and Merak SS, all the rest amid shippers.

For this, he went to the man and company he referred to as "the best in the business"—Italian designer Giorgetto Giugiaro and his Italdesign firm in Turin, Italy. After tenures at stalwart Italian design houses and coachbuilders Ghia and Bertone, Giugiaro formed Italdesign.

His portfolio of mid-engined, exotic cars is definitive, including the De Tomaso Mangusta, Maserati's Bora and Merak SS production designs and the groundbreaking Boomerang concept car, the Lotus Esprit, BMW M1, plus many more concepts and design studies. When it comes to mid-engined exotics, not to mention many seminal designs that are not mid-engined, Giugiaro is "The Man."

Opposite, top: John DeLorean left his metaphorical fingerprints on many cars along the GM trail, but DMC represented the first time his name would literally be *on* the car. Italdesign created all of the car's badging, graphics, and logotypes. *Italdesign photo.*
Opposite, bottom: Some of Italdesign's earliest ideation renderings already began to set the tone of the shapes and proportions that would become of the final DMC-12. The major differences here is that this rendering features hideaway headlights, but the gullwing doors and rear sail panels are already extant. *Italdesign photo*

3

Opposite, top: Maserati's Merak SS had a lot in common with the proposed DeLorean including its general size and proportions, V-6 power, and Italdesign DNA parenthood. It also wore steel and aluminum bodywork and no gullwing doors. **Opposite, bottom:** The Maserati Boomerang concept car was Italdesign's much edgier and updated take on the original ethos of the previous production Bora and Merak. The creases are much sharper, and the split glass in the doors is an innovative and exciting look. *Italdesign photo.* **Right:** The DeTomaso Mangusta is a mid-engined, exotic masterpiece of design, done while Mr. Giugiaro worked at Carrozzeria Ghia. Its proportions are nigh to perfect, its flanks and panels clean, and it used gullwing doors over the rear-engine bay instead of the passenger doors. It also employed a center spine chassis design, as did the Lotus Esprit and would the final DMC-12, but in this execution, the chassis lacked structural rigidity, which caused far too much chassis flex. But it's as pretty as it gets. *Wikimedia photo*

No designer nor design house had more success with Italian mid-engined exotic car design than Italdesign.

DeLorean had already ideated several key styling/design elements that were to be integral elements of the makeup of His Car. Chief among them was the use of gullwing-style doors. He was said to have been considering prospective safety engineering benefits of the wider door sills possibly afforded by this layout, potentially adding increased crash protection in the event of a mid-car side impact. The deeper sill and rocker panel areas could also allow space to engineer in additional chassis rigidity. The real driver for this mandate, however, was how exotic and exciting this design touch is and that it would surely become a trademark calling card for the new DeLorean machine. Mercedes-Benz had previously deployed gullwing doors to great effect on successful racing and street versions of its then extremely exotic 300 SL Gullwing coupe models. The Bricklin SV-1, a front-engined, fiberglass bodied gullwing doored GT coupe introduced in 1974 had recently failed in the marketplace, but not for reasons related to this door design or cockpit layout. DeLorean wanted them, so gullwing-style doors it would be.

From the beginning, based on Giugiaro's first sketches and renderings, the DeLorean sports coupe was a pure two-seater. DeLorean chose to avoid the temptation of squeezing in a pair of near useless "jump seats" between the front seats and the engine. In mid- and rear-engine designs, rear passenger compartment seating is also a serious compromise, the resultant area often ending up useful only as a package shelf. This is obvious in the Porsche 911, where the rear squab of the back seat folds down to create a flat parcel deck, and most 911 owners tend to keep it folded down this way at all or most times, seldom thinking of attempting to fold an adult with legs into this area. Another example of how this concept didn't really work as meaningful seating is

Giugiaro's own Maserati Merak—beautiful machine though it is, there's a near worthless pair of miniscule jump seats squeezed between the backs of the front seats and the bulkhead separating the engine bay and passenger compartment. So, this first DeLorean product would be for two only, with ideas and notions about more seating held up for future projects, as we'll discuss later.

Another engineering/design touch that the boss insisted on was the use of stainless steel body panels. They would not only provide an exceptionally unique and exotic look, but would also minimize planned obsolescence in terms of virtually eliminating body panel rot through and also discourage the whim and trends of paint color offerings. This construction has been tried and done before, to varying levels of success. The most notable early examples of this approach date to a joint program between Ford and the Alleghany Ludlam Steel Corporation, which built a trio of interesting prototypes to evaluate the

Lotus was a logical choice to production-engineer the DeLorean, as the company had meaningful experience with the central spine chassis layout, and with Italdesign.

viability and realities of full stainless steel body work. The first fruit of this joint project was a 1936 Ford Tudor 2-Door sedan. Based on cost estimates and the need for different stamps and dies than used for conventional mild steel, this mid-1930s project went no further at the time, although the car racked up high mileage with little issue related to the shiny metal.

This direction went quiet for Ford during WWII, although the Blue Oval and Alleghany reconvened on the idea for 1960 with a stainless paneled '60 Ford Thunderbird coupe, although it must be said that more and more stainless trim began showing up on a variety of cars in the 1950s. Certain top-level Pontiacs had brushed stainless trim panels running down their flanks, and the largely handbuilt, and the very expensive, Cadillac Eldorado Brougham of 1957–1958 employed a brushed stainless steel roof panel. The T-Bird took the whole notion a step further in that its grille, bumpers, and body panels were made of type 302 stainless steel. According to Silodrome's Gasoline Culture website, "stainless steel is a blanket term for steel alloys that contain approximately 11% chromium (commonly referred to as chrome). Steel is made by mixing iron with carbon, and stainless steel is made by adding chromium to the mix, though other metals are also frequently used resulting in hundreds of varieties of stainless-steel alloy with varying strengths and weaknesses."

The final entry into the Ford/Alleghany scrapbook was large, imposing, and elegant 1966 Lincoln Continental Convertible sedan of which three were built. The big Continental ragtop was trimmed in a delft blue leather interior with a dark blue top and is a dazzling if flashily elegant sight. This was an interesting experiment as this generation of Continental was not a ladder or perimeter frame type car (with separate body on frame construction) but instead a unibody layout, where the bodywork is depended on for structural strength and rigidity of the entire platform. It also turned out that 1967 was the final year for the Continental convertible sedan body style, so in essence, other than to evaluate the materials usage, the idea of a production version was practically stillborn.

One aspect of the projected DeLorean car's layout that somewhat favored the use of stainless is that John wanted the car's body to rest on a composite chassis, so the bodywork wouldn't be stressed, structural elements of the chassis, as it would be in a unibody/monocoque sports car.

One of the materials' potential risks is brittleness, depending on the specific metal's metallurgical makeup. The same is true for the metal's corrosion resistance. Some stainless metals are so highly blended with certain properties that they really are virtually stainless under nearly any condition. This is often referred to as "surgical" stainless for obvious reasons. Lower grade blends can still corrode. And in most cases, it takes tougher stronger (more expensive) stamps and dies to shape stainless steel panels and/or more strikes or hits of the stamping equipment to create a certain shape. This would be addressed in the car's engineering and production.

Giugiaro got busy straightway and created a basic shape, along with many themes and variations, of John's vision for his ultimate ethical grand touring sports car, incorporating of course rear-engine placement, gullwing-style doors, and a brushed stainless steel skin. Giugiaro and DeLorean appeared closely aligned on each other's vision for this car, as once the basic envelop was established, much of the rest of the work consisted of production-feasible detail work including windows, lighting, badging, wheel design, and the cabin.

Given Italdesign's experience and success designing mid-engined exotica, it's no surprise that the initial DeLorean shapes were exciting and well proportioned. In as much as so many automotive designs up and down the spectrum were evolving toward square sealed beam headlamps, the DeLorean wore two of them per side, from the beginning. The taillight cluster designs had a certain high-tech, computerized look about them. The logotypes and lettering were also a modernistic, rounded block font that fit the time and the car. One particular design challenge of the gullwing doors was how to best incorporate a window, for both ventilation and "fast food drive-through" access, as this type of door can't accommodate a full-sized glass window. Giugiaro's solution was brilliant, that being smallish round edged triangular "toll booth" windows which quickly power up and down as needed.

Although all manner of the mid- and rear-engine machines could be said to have lent something to the DeLorean's design, it still came off as fresh,

Right: Mercedes-Benz made gullwing sports cars famous in the 1950s and updated the notion for a modern series of wing-doored concept cars in the 1960s and 70s, called C-111, of which there were three. John DeLorean had great affection for Mercedes-Benz design, engineering, and quality ethos, so this mid-engined C-111/II of 1970 was certainly on his radar. You'll notice its general vibe is somewhat similar to the DMC-12's, especially in terms of the glassed-in rear buttresses.

unique, individual, exotic, and exciting. It is to DeLorean and Giugiaro's credit that this can still be said many decades beyond when it was conceived. DeLorean was very hands-on during this process, visiting the Italdesign studios in Turin throughout the design process. Giugiaro, no stranger to high-powered automotive execs, couldn't help but be impressed with DeLorean's size, physical character, and big personality, affectionately nicknaming him "Mr. Hollywood."

The same group and company would also develop the interior. Many renderings and much clay modeling were done to crystallize the look, feel, and safety-inspired nature of Mr. DeLorean's ethical sports car. A netted storage area was designed just aft of the seats. A comprehensive modular instrument was positioned straight ahead of the driver, with ancillary controls and a Craig audio system in the dash's center stack and some controls on the center console around the shifter.

Above: Ford again created stainless steel bodied prototypes: in 1960 with a Ford Thunderbird and in 1966 with this huge, and assuredly heavy, 1966 Lincoln Continental Convertible. The convertible Continental body style was gone by 1968, and its trademark "suicide" center opening doors by 1970. *Ford Media Archive photo*

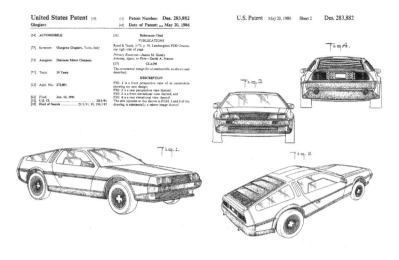

Above: The original Henry Ford had an eye on the values of stainless steel bodywork as far as the mid-1930s. This Allegheny/Ludlam steel paneled '36 Ford not only looked great but was tested for many tens of thousands of miles (kilometers) and served well, proving the material's worth for car bodies. *Ford Media Archive photo.*

Right: It's official! This is one element of Italdesign's patent application for the DMC-12. The date of this document is a bit curious (May 1986) as the car and the company were both out of business by that point. *Italdesign photo*

In the earliest days of the company, the management team and employee roster were relatively thin, logical in that they weren't yet building cars, and it only makes sense to watch salary costs before the company is earning income. So, DeLorean needed to fill a variety of management positions. They then needed to add staff to deal with the legion of chores in designing and production engineering a new car and company from scratch, including building a new factory property from nearly the ground up.

There isn't need to mention every single employee that ever joined DeLorean, but this is a good juncture to highlight some of the major hires. In no particular order:

Engineer Bill Collins was a John DeLorean team auto industry vet of some years and accomplishment, and a long time DeLorean confidant going back to his days at Pontiac. Collins could design/engineer the seemingly smallest pieces or components on any automobile or lead teams of people to make an entire car—which in this case initially was his primary responsibility. He also led the charge in getting the earliest vehicle designs from Giugiaro into virtually handbuilt models and running prototypes, which we'll get to in a bit.

Another Michigan transplant was Eugene "Gene" Cafiero who came in as DMC president in 1978, the man on the front line of company management just below John DeLorean. A serious industry vet with a deep resume, he was for a time Chrysler president just prior to Lee Iacocca, through some of its darker days. Cafiero also did some time at Ford, so he was a qualified all-rounder.

Barrie Wills, who ultimately became DMC's longest tenured employee, a highly educated and experienced automotive industry exec, joined as director

of purchasing and went on to become director of supplies and director of product development and supply. That multifaceted umbrella title covers a lot of ground, getting everything in the door in order to make cars and get them out the door. Dick Brown came aboard as VP of sales and marketing and generally oversaw the company's US operations. Bob Dewey was the original Chief Financial Officer (CFO), then Walt Strycker 1979–1980, Jim Stark (1980–1981), and then Joe Daly (1981–1982).

Public and Media relations is an important function in any company, but particularly a start-up and just as particularly a car company—there are lots of financial and other sorts of newspapers and magazine, automotive magazines, and buyer's guides who test vehicles and write reviews. In the pre-Internet days, positive reviews in influential car magazines could make or break a car, as happened many times in automotive history. John DeLorean came in contact with veteran motojourno Mike Knepper during the latter's tenure making the round of the Big Four auto titles, including *Road & Track*, *Car and Driver*, *MotorTrend*, and *Autoweek*. Knepper joined the DeLorean Motor Company in 1980 as the PR Director, working directly for DeLorean.

Jerry Williamson came along as promotions manager, while bringing with him a notable career in automotive design—he would be a good eye and voice on the DMC side of the relationship with Italdesign. Jerry was primarily in charge of prepping scale models, prototypes, and production cars

WHO IS ITALDESIGN?

ITALDESIGN

Above: The ever-handsome Giugiaro speaks very little English but seems to understand it very well. No matter, he's a world master in the universal language of great design work, particularly cars. His portfolio includes not only exotic sports and luxury cars, but simpler, harder working designs such as the original Fiat Panda and Volkswagen Golf Rabbit. Anytime a list of all-time great automotive designers is drawn up, his name as very near—or at—the top as perhaps the greatest ever to put pen to automotive paper. *Italdesign photo.*
Right: The Italdesign logo is modern and dynamic and often appears on many products that the company designs, be they automobiles, bullet trains, food bottling, industrial equipment, or whatever. It's a design brand people recognize and still ensures thoughtful, quality design work internationally. *Italdesign photo*

For decades, Italy has been the epicenter of creative, expressive, innovative, and often exciting transportation design. That isn't to say for a moment that the United States, England, Germany, or France haven't provided the shapes and inspirations for so many of the world's most compelling cars. Yet, legions of the great masterworks, particularly those many label "Exotics," were born in the minds of gifted Italian industrial and transportation designers.

Most are names that in-the-know automotive afficionados are moderately to keenly aware of: Pininfarina, Zagato, Ghia, Michelotti, Frua, and Bertone. And, some would say, sitting atop that considerable heap is Giorgetto Giugiaro. The handsome, affable, and perennially enthusiastic Giugiaro (pronounced *Jew-JAR-Oh*, the latter being the most phonetically accurate way to describe the pronunciation of his name, even though he is not Jewish) was born in 1938 Garessio, Italy, a suburb of large, industrial Turin, often referred to as *Torino* in Italian. Although he's best known for car design, he's also a superbly multidimensional industrial designer that has designed cameras, wristwatches, furniture, the *tradizionale* round bottomed balsamic vinegar bottle, Italy's bullet trains, pasta, and even a 7,000-pipe cathedral organ. His considerable career path included significant stints at Fiat, Bertone, and Ghia prior to hanging his proverbial shingle and forming Italdesign Giugiaro in Turin. And his automotive portfolio includes far more than strictly the "fast and dangerous" exotic type cars. He's designed buses and trucks, the original and decidedly humble Fiat Panda, several Volkswagens, taxi concepts—anything with wheels and an engine was fair game for his discerning eye and pen.

No designer has done more—or better—mid-engine low slung exotic car designs than has Giugiaro, and that made him a solid, logical choice by John DeLorean as his car's design partner. Many consider Mr. Giugiaro as the GOAT among automotive designers—including John DeLorean, who once referred to him as "the best in the business." ∎

for what he called "DeLorean's dog and pony shows" where the car would be introduced to dealers, investors, and at the auto shows. They had to look great, light up, and shine—literally and figuratively—next to John DeLorean on stage or on camera.

Other names of note will emerge as they enter at given points in the story, but this core team filled key spots on the org chart, building the company and thus the cars.

John DeLorean had an idea, some money, an executive staff, and a plot of land in Northern Ireland. It was time to build a factory, in order to build his car.

As described by Barrie Wills in *John Z, the DeLorean & Me*: "On July 28, 1978, after 45 days of consideration, the Industrial Development Corporation for Northern Ireland, a branch of the Northern Ireland Office of the Government of the United Kingdom agreed to a 65 million pounds Stirling investment package. [Just] Two days later, a new company, DeLorean Motor Cars Limited (DMCL) moved onto a vacant 72-acre [291,374 m2] site, in Dunmurry, West Belfast. It contained a disused carpet warehouse and a large empty country house known as The Warren House. Other than that, it was a rough 'cow pasture' divided by two meandering brooks cutting right through the DeLorean property—hence the name of the bordering housing estate—Twinbrook."

Mr. Wills continues: "At this time, many parts of Northern Ireland were a near war zone and West Belfast itself a hive of warring factions. The site for the new car assembly plant was bordered on one side by the aforementioned Republican Twinbrook housing estate and on the other—across the main railway line from Belfast to Dublin—by the Loyalist Seymour Hill estate."

As the Brits might say, it was "time to get cracking" with architects, industrial building contractors, and big earthmoving equipment.

Charles K. "Chuck" Bennington was DMCL's first managing director from 1978–1980 and took a major role in leading the charge of constructing the DeLorean plant and factory facilities, on the company's behalf. His fingerprints are on most of the factory property and on so much of what the DeLorean cars became. And it would be a very different sort of operation than the dusty, smoke belching industrial monsters that John DeLorean had spent so many years at while at General Motors. Some of the functions and facilities at the Belfast property were by necessity heavy industrial places and activities, while others were clean, efficient, well lighted, modern, and downright quiet by comparison. Final assembly in traditional vehicle plants involves a train track–style "assembly line" that Henry Ford became so famous for popularizing in the industry, although he did not invent it. DeLorean's would be much different. After certain stages of production where a body/chassis/tub unit began looking much like a car, each united "floated" across the assembly floors on a motorized Tellus carrier unit from area to area.

DeLorean sales materials discussed this philosophy far more than would normally be found in the typical automobile sales brochure: "The DeLorean Motor Cars Limited assembly plant is situated on a carefully planned 72-acre [291,374 m2] site in Dunmurry, North Ireland. Five major structures compris-

John DeLorean wanted his car's cabin to be luxuriously sporty, if not bare bones racey. So rich leather everwhere was a fundamental design touch.

ing more than 650,000 square feet [60,387 m2] have been designed and equipped exclusively for the assembly and testing of the DeLorean. But extensive use of advanced production technology is not the only distinction.

Worker environment was a special consideration at the DeLorean plant, from initial design through to production. Unlike the traditional assembly method in which each worker repeats a single, monotonous task again, and again, DeLorean employees perform several different jobs as members of a team. The absence of congestion and assembly line pits add to a pleasant working atmosphere. This extra attention to the personal satisfaction and pride of accomplishment of the DeLorean labor force is clearly reflected in a most tangible way; the consistently superior quality of workmanship you can expect to find in every DeLorean."

There were ostensibly two project managers of the design, architecture, engineering, and construction of the DeLorean property—American Dixon Hollinshead, who had experience in the design and construction of automotive

Below: Deeply gathered "bunched" leather was very common and popular for Italian cars, particularly luxury or sport models, in the 1970s and 1980s, so it only made sense that this look would be evaluated. *Italdesign photo*

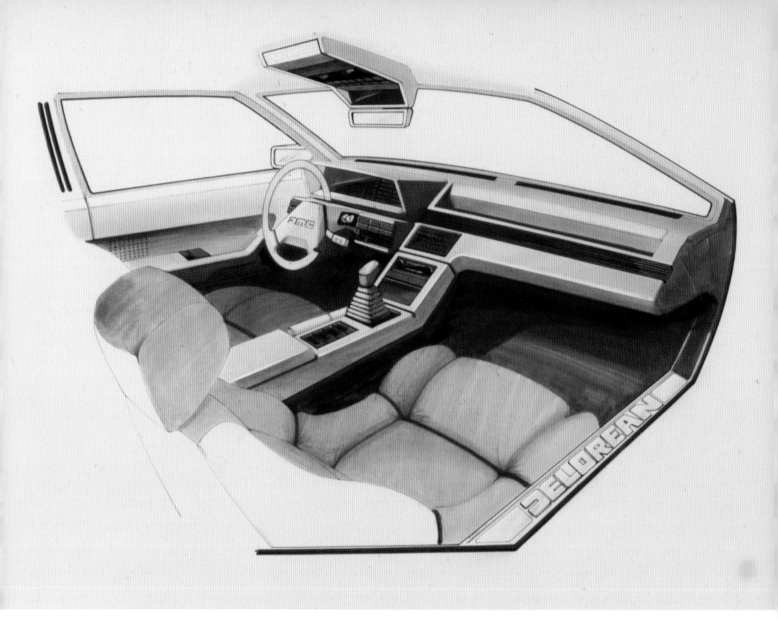

Above: Italdesign created many concept renderings for the DeLorean cabin. It's interesting to note that even in this early illustration, DMC is visibly stamped into the steering wheel boss, and there's a wide, leg and knee safety pad running the width of the cabin at the bottom edge of the dash. *Italdesign photo*

construction and distribution properties, and on-site managing director Chuck Bennington. Two Northern Ireland construction contractors worked in joint venture on DeLorean: Farrans Construction of local Dunmurry and McLaughlin & Harvey of Newtownabbey. Local JMJ civil engineers handled much of the on-site engineering work and detailing, while local architectural firm Brodie & Hawthorn were the principal designers. In order to shave time off of the often-elongated schedules of such major construction, each new phase of construction frequently began prior to the completion of a previous process. This was described as a parallel construction approach.

Prepping the site for construction was no small job, as it was not only very large, but needed considerable work to be able to hold the weight of

Above: Here's proof that a variety of instrument pod designs were considered. This unit came out of some other car entirely, evidenced by the clock at right instead of a tachometer and the speedometer's 180 kilometers per hour (112 mph) top speed. *Italdesign photo*

the central production buildings, steelwork, glass, and production equipment. Primary project managers Bennington, Hollinshead, and senior architect Hawthorn got right to it overseeing the rerouting of the previously "twin brooks" waterways, which cut right through the middle of the property. These natural waterways were redeveloped into underground rivers, which avoided the wasting of valuable ground level acreage. Because most of the property was a waterlogged and somewhat soggy bog, much deep re-grading was required, as well as the laying down of stone aggregate to stabilize the ground. Five main structures were initially envisioned for the body shop, assembly shop, emissions testing, and final vehicle preparation and finish. They also required training and office space, plus an onsite vehicle and performance dynamics test track facility. All of this activity brought substantial investment and employment opportunities.

Heavy construction began in early 1979 with all of the earth moving and aggregate laying, with steel framework of several of the massive buildings already visible on the property's skyline by that summer. Also of critical importance from a local point-of-pride and also outside appearances standpoint was the construction of a handsome entry and main gate area welcoming any-

Left, Opposite: Building design models out of clay is the dirty, messy, stinky part of vehicle design, and even though today's modern computer-aided design (CAD) milling machines can mill an entire car model out of a block of foam, handlaid clay was still the absolute method of choice in the early 1980s, and at some design studios, remains so today. *Italdesign photos*

one to the property, featuring a more than prominent DMC signage and lush landscaping. DMCL Dunmurry would soon be welcoming its local workforce and open for business.

Meanwhile, as the factory was being funded, designed, constructed, and outfitted, the ideation, design, and engineering of the DMC car continued. Static models and rolling prototypes also needed to be created.

Italdesign presented an initial DeLorean design concept, along with several variations on the primary theme in terms of certain details—such as window treatments (particularly those for the gullwing doors), wheel designs, lighting and grille styles, and other variables. There were also the "little considerations," such as suspension layout and components, and the sourcing and testing of an entire powertrain, and the need for the team to build some models and prototypes.

From the very beginning, the DeLorean designers, engineers, and management team had always intended to outsource its engine and transaxle supply needs. As with so many tasks at this early stage of the game, powertrain evaluation, testing, and development fell squarely on the shoulders of Chief Engineer Bill Collins, as well as the construction of at least one non-running model for use at car shows, dealer events, and such, plus engineering prototypes to shake out and finalize every engineering-related aspect and decision ultimately translating to production cars.

The car's hardware and engineering parameters were clearly understood between Collins and DeLorean, the notion as described in John Lamm's *De Lorean: Stainless Steel Illusion* being a "gentleman's sports car with

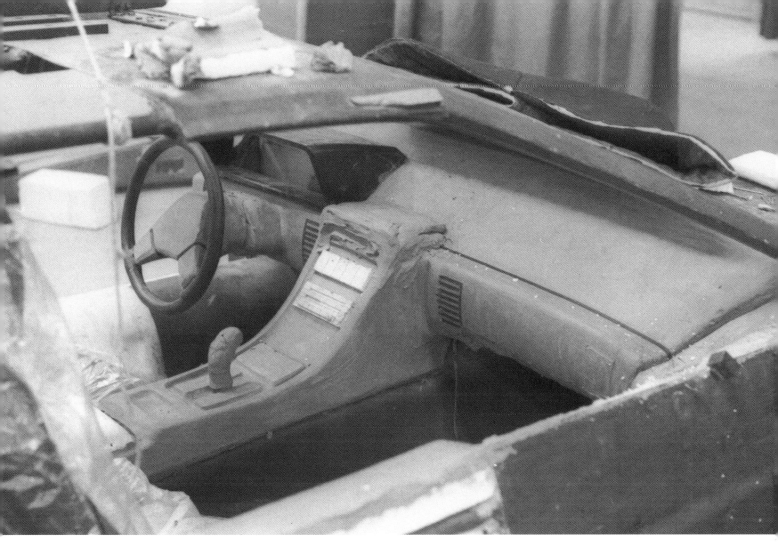

dramatic styling, a rear-mounted engine, stainless steel bodywork, gullwing doors, a sporty, well-appointed cabin for two, reasonable fuel economy, and good performance." The old engineering buddies (together at GM with Pontiac) equally agreed that the car be a responsibly designed "ethical sports car," meaning a high degree of safety and good fuel economy and not destined to be the sort of vehicle that would be obsolete and unusable in very few years. DeLorean abhorred the notion of "planned obsolescence" so prevalent at the Detroit carmakers.

One of the benefits of the stainless steel skin would be rust and corrosion resistance (drive through Michigan and you'll see all manner of vehicles with rotted out rocker and lower door panels often with rusty fenders flapping in the breeze). This also led to solutions such as the intended composite chassis construction and plastic fuel tanks. DeLorean wanted his car to last no matter where it lived and be economical to maintain and repair. Another important design parameter was the ability to comfortably house tallish drivers and

passengers—DeLorean was 6 feet 4 inches (1.9 m) and Collins was just an inch (2.5 centimeters [cm]) less, so they had the perfect seating and headroom models directly in-house.

Before they even got to models and design prototypes, there was a considerable amount of powertrain consideration and evaluation going on, while Italdesign was still finalizing design details (inside and outside of the cabin). DeLorean had initially fancied a then revolutionary Wankel rotary engine for his new sports car, which made some sense on the surface—the engine philosophy was innovative, somewhat simple from an engineering standpoint, smooth running, offered good power at high revs, and was relatively light. GM had invested millions in rotary engine development, even building a pair of very attractive rotary powered Corvette design studies, which DeLorean was familiar with as all of this activity took place during his time at GM. One of them in fact used a four-rotor prototype engine, mounted in the back of an

Above: This early concept panel is interesting in many ways, as the front end somewhat emulates what the DeLorean would become, while the rear aspect angle less so. The side view reminds us very much of the Lancia Beta Montecarlo (Lancia Beta Scorpion in the United States), which is purely coincidental, as the Lancia was designed at Pininfarina. *Italdesign photo*

Above: What became the DMC-12's front end ethos is becoming more familiar in this rendering, although the side view, partic ularly in the window and rear deck lines, is decidedly more BMW M1. *Italdesign photo*

exotic looking Corvette prototype that feature gullwing doors (although no stainless steel skin), all of which spoke to the ideas DeLorean had in mind for his car. Ultimately, GM binned its rotary engine development plans, leaving Mazda and NSU to use these engines in production cars.

Collins shopped about for other engine alternatives, becoming very interested in Ford's 2.8-liter (170.9 cu in), 60-degree "even-fire" V-6 as employed in the Ford/Mercury Capri and a variety of other English and other world market Ford models. This seemed a worthwhile choice, as the engine was durable and smooth running, made good power (about 120 horsepower [88 kW] in carbureted, naturally aspirated form), could be turbocharged for higher output models, and wasn't too heavy nor overly expensive to buy. Recently joining Collins' team, as a Detroit-based independent contractor, was Mike Pocobello, a former GM engineer who had some experience with the Texas-based Chaparral racing team. Pocobello set about constructing what

1

may in some ways be considered the first DeLorean engineering prototype, although it looked nothing like a DeLorean.

Metaphorically speaking, he had a 2.8-liter (170.9 cu in) Ford V-6 in one hand and a tiny, mid-engine Fiat X1/9 in the other. He shoehorned the engine and a five-speed Borg-Warner manual transmission into the back to the pint-sized Italian sports car, connecting the engine and transmission together via a bit of a Rube Goldbergesque chain drive system.

Much of the X1/9s externals remained stock because the build was only to assess powertrain viability. Yet, it wore a couple of highly distinctive, and unusual, exterior treatments that immediately gave away that this was no standard X1/9. Early engineering analysis disclosed that the DeLorean's anticipated heavily rearward weight bias could result in unpredictable, if not dangerous, oversteer tendencies. Porsche had battled with this "tailhappy" notion since the 911s development in the early 1960s. Besides ongoing suspension refinement and evolution, one important way Porsche's engineers dealt with this problem is tire stagger, meaning in this case that the car would wear larger, rolling stock in the rear than in the front. So, Pocobello bolted a pair of oversized aftermarket aluminum mag wheels to the rear of the X1/9 monster wearing large, sticky, Pirelli P7 tires and left the Fiat's standard narrow 13-inch (15 cm) wheels and tires up front, simulating the stagger affect needed to hopefully balance the anticipated oversteer handling that the heavier

Above: Now, we begin to see the DMC-12s shapes and surface detail beginning to come together more concisely. The front end is much more similarly realized, as are the gullwing doors and fender flares. It's all a process. *Italdesign photo.* **Opposite:** This concept ultimately had very little to do with what became the DeLorean. It's much smaller and doesn't have gullwing doors, although the front end angle is closer to the other views. *Italdesign photo*

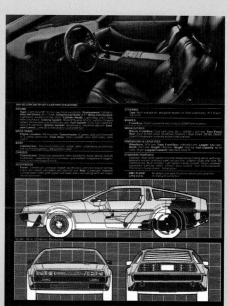

MARKETING THE DREAM, AND THE CAR

Caption: DeLorean's marketing materials were lush and clean looking, emphasizing the silver and black theme of a car with a stainless steel skin and a gray and black leather interior.

An old saw in the sales game, particularly of cars, jewelry, and appliances was to "sell the sizzle, not the steak." It would be entirely unfair to characterize the DMC-12 as a sizzle-only machine, as there was more than enough steak there to appeal to a variety of appetites. Yet, the sales materials, brochures, and advertising, and other sales and marketing related properties featured lush glossy photos of the DeLorean in rich, elegant places (at the harbor, parked in front of charming restaurants, or at the airport docked up by a private plane or helicopter) and a good number of them featured John DeLorean himself or at least a handsome young couple, looking longingly at the car and each other. There's nothing wrong with any of this, as the purveyors of luxury goods have done so for decades. Look at many carmakers' similar materials and advertising and marketing creative and you'll see the same, and a lot of it: Corvette, Porsche, Jaguar, and even Ferrari now and again. Many such materials encouraged the buyer to *Live the Dream*. John DeLorean, having a lot of exposure and experience to advertising and marketing companies seeking multimillion dollar advertising contracts, realized the value of such materials and campaigns, yet was in some ways a bit conservative in promoting the car as too much or only in his image. He was also careful to do advertising tie-in programs with companies that contributed to the company or bolstered its image. They include Craig, which provided the car's audio systems, Sylvania (halogen headlights), Goodyear (NCT high-performance tires), and Cutty Sark Scotch. The company's customer handout sales materials were very tech looking and conservative, often featuring a black and white theme emphasizing the car's design, unique construction, technology, and bespoke manufacturing. ∎

Above: Excepting the funky stripes, the DMC-12's form is now clearly formed in this very early design model. Of course, the unusual wheel styling had nothing to do with the final form, although this chunky design was very popular at the time, and Italdesign employed it on a number of its concept cars. Note the fuel filler aperture appearing on the top rear of the driver's side front fender, instead of up at the hood-line. *Italdesign photo*

rear-mounted powertrain would likely create. The X1/9 is technically a mid-engined car, but as the DeLorean was shaping up with more of a rear-engine bias, the Ford engine was also installed in the Fiat aft of the rear axle line. As the beefy rear rubber seal stuck out about six inches (15 cm) proud of the Fiat's svelte door stop–shaped body, the team added an ungainly looking, but functional, pair of black metal (or plastic) bolt-on fenders that would easily look at home on a small U-Haul trailer.

Another ungainly but functional bit of hardware that was needed to keep the V-6 intake system inside of the X 1/9's body panels was the addition of a sort of snail-shaped black metal (or more likely plastic) housing mounted atop the rear decklid to encompass the higher deck height of the Ford's intake manifold, carburetor, and air filter plumbing.

Pocobello designed and fabbed the much-modified rear suspension, transmission chain drive, and everything else needed to shoehorn the Ford six- and five-speed gearbox into the aft end of the diminutive Fiat. It sure wasn't pretty but had a weight-to-power ratio far exceeding that served up by the X1/9s 1300cc I-4. It was said to be fast and in that case, fun to drive, but the chain drive setup was a temporary solution, not one ideally suited to a production scenario. On one particularly spirited test run with Pocobello at the wheel, the homebuilt transfer case spilled its guts all over the freeway, and the "Red Rocket's" days as a legit DeLorean development vehicle were pretty much over.

Lest we forget that during all the exploration of powertrain alternatives, final design details of the car were still being massaged by Giugiaro in Turin. Recall DeLorean's strong desire to incorporate the ERM to create a lightweight, corrosion-resistant composite chassis "tub" for his car. Once more serious hands-on product development began regarding the use of ERM for the chassis, the more roadblocks that seemed to present themselves. The technology was certainly innovative, using moldable upper and lower fiberglass sheets with urethane foam sandwiched between. Yet, this was only at the time feasible for the lower tub of the passenger compartment and underfloors of the chassis. It was not yet viable for the upper structure of the passenger compartment, nor capable of mounting the gullwing doors. It wasn't long before the team came to grips with the notion that the car needed a steel chassis that could underpin a composite floor tube and passenger cell.

In order to advance the design and construction of running prototypes, the team settled on a 2.0-liter (122.0 cu in) inline four-cylinder engine found in the production front-wheel drive Citroen CX2000 sedan that could be acquired from Citroen at a reasonable price and in adequate volume should it be decided upon as a final choice for the production DeLorean. One immediate and potentially long-term benefit of such a choice was that the Citroen I-4 was already production engineered to be transversely mounted in a front-wheel drive car and came with its own four-speed manual transmission attached. While hardly dazzling from a power output standpoint, it seemed a logical choice to get the engine compartment and rear suspension of the car sorted out.

Some of the earliest of Italdesign's mock-ups and models looked a bit too much like some of its own offspring, cars like the BMW M1 and Lotus Esprit. DeLorean and Collins visited Turin often to hone and refine the design shapes and surface detailing for the right look and uniqueness that they sought. One thing that most Italian design houses are extremely capable of is churning out a significant number of mock-ups and models in very short order incorporating the latest round of updates and changes, and Giugiaro did that for DeLorean. The shapes of the window glass, bumpers, lighting, badging, wheels, and myriad other design points were honed and refined countlessly in a short period of time, resulting in something that very much resembled the final production model.

This also included the hand fabrication of several interior design bucks detailing every nuance of the seating, door and dash panels, console, controls, and controls placement, down to instrument design, gauge faces, and shifters.

DeLorean and Collins were involved in every one of these decisions and monitored the balance of the design process in a very eyes- and hands-on manner. Major engineering decisions still remained, including the finalization of the chassis design and materials, a production ready power- and drivetrain, and countless supplier component resolutions.

In the meantime, however, investors, employees, the company's British government financiers, and the automotive media wanted to see *wunderkind* John DeLorean's new car, so a running prototype was the next order of business. Prototyping is a very specialized business, and there are a variety of companies around the world qualified for the job.

It is somewhat amazing, although not procedurally unusual, as to how the detailing of the DMC-12 evolved from the very earliest drawings and scale models.

Opposite top: Here's one of the full-sized design mock-ups being shaved out of a giant block of clay or foam. Most of the design's hardpoints are clearly already in place. *Italdesign photo*

Mike Pocobello's company, TRIAD, was primarily on point to put together the first running DeLorean prototype that actually resembled what the real production DMC-12 would look like, but this isn't a project undertaken in one's garage or backyard. So Pocobello and Collins engaged Detroit area–based Kar Kraft for this one-off, specialized build, using some number of components contributed by the actual DeLorean suppliers and the rest either being hand-built or sourced from other vehicles, companies, or users. Kar Kraft is a highly capable, specialized "job shop" that builds prototypes, engineering vehicles, and has over time built many historic big game racing cars, primarily although not exclusively Fords. The company administrated the short run production lines used to produce the Ford Mustang Boss 302 and Boss 429 Mustangs. For them, building a single DeLorean prototype is the proverbial walk in the park.

This singular job required a considerable amount of bespoke fabrication, including a frame and subframes, a handlaid fiberglass floor and passenger compartment (remember that the ERM chassis plan was out at this point), plus a steel "spider structure" for mounting the gullwing doors, and a virtually hand-crafted interior. The car would run the aforementioned transversely mounted Cit-roen 2-liter (122 cu in) I-4 engine and its attendant four-speed manual transaxle.

So, this car would appear much more of a runner than some concept car prototypes that earn the not necessarily complimentary terms "golf cart"

Above: This early prototype has a very different and more chiseled front bumper/fascia design and a caramel/butterscotch leather interior—something that never made it onto production DMC-12s. We don't know the date or location of this display, but the car just behind appears to be a production DMC-12. Even though initial engineering chief Bill Collins suffered a somewhat bitter departure from the company, he remained very proud of his work and of the car, even at the end lamenting that "they should have put the tan interior in it." *Paul Briden/Alamy Stock photo.*

Opposite, Right: One design element the early "Epowood model" (left and right) had in common with its Maserati Merak SS cousin was the notion of unglassed and unslatted flying buttresses visually extending the rear deckline from the aft portion of the roof, touching down at the rear corners of the deck. The look served the Maserati well but was vetoed and became a glassed-in panel on the DeLorean. *Italdesign photos*

because even though the vehicle may look like a fully realized running car, many such mock-ups and turntable toys are powered by batteries and electric golf cart motors. The car that Kar Kraft would assemble was to use as many production specs as were finalized and could be provided by suppliers—there were still details that would change and evolve, such as the shapes of some glass and window panels, various stainless steel stampings, and countless interior details, yet for all the world it looked like a real live DeLorean DMC-12. And under the bright lights at an auto show or dealer convention, when the cool and confident looking John Z. DeLorean opened up those fabulous doors or drove the car onto a stage or into a room, the fact that it wasn't yet a fully realized production car yet didn't matter.

It looked close enough and dazzled everywhere it went. Another running prototype was also constructed, as was a display-only model made of epowood, which is a wood product imbued with large amounts of epoxy to make it formable and strong (often used in furniture-making).

Meanwhile, Back in Belfast

Building a virtually all new, from the ground up factory from an essentially greenfield site in strife torn Dunmurry was no easy feat, yet was undertaken with optimism and zeal at all levels. The physicality of the property presented its own challenges, such as having to redirect the flow of river water, along with dealing with contractors and laborers who'd never constructed an automobile factory before. No matter, a groundbreaking ceremony was held at the DeLorean factory site on October 2, 1978, with a commitment to being ready to volume produce cars for the 1981 model year—functionally in approximately two years' time. There was a bit of protesting held outside the factory gates, which did nothing to shake management's decision to locate and produce its cars in Northern Ireland.

This aggressive timeline had to include not only building the property out in terms of structures and systems, but also equipping it with the infrastructure to produce cars, all of the various supplier contracts and product development, and the hiring and training of employees, factory workers, and management.

Productionizing the DeLorean

Even as the prototypes were being developed, hand finished, and bandied about in the media and the Dunmurry factory was under construction, the DMC-12 was hardly ready for prime time.

The searches continued for viable powertrain solutions, a high-tech yet producible chassis structure, and the right entity to production engineer the car. The use of the 1985cc Citroen inline four and its attendant transaxle in the first prototype made sense as it was expedient, and the package size and configuration made for a generally straightforward installation in the back of the De-Lorean. Although, for an upscale grand touring sports car such as the DMC-12, its 102 horsepower (75 kW) output wasn't nearly enough, and the four-speed manual transmission wasn't market competitive against the five-speeds offered

Actor Alec Baldwin would later portray John DeLorean in a documentary film. Even though JDZ is a few inches taller than Baldwin, the resemblance is striking, hair and makeup magic not withstanding.

Opposite: In a more meaningful ground-breaking gesture than simply turning over dirt with gold painted shovels, the DeLoreans and others planted three trees, reputedly representing the coming together of local Catholic and Protestant locals with their new bosses and teammates from America. *Alexx Michael Archive photo.*

Above: The Dunmurry Big Picture. The aerial view at lower left gives an idea of how the factory grounds were laid out and the relative size of the 75 or so acre (30,3514 m2) property. The onsite test track is visible at lower right, and the other photos give a look inside at the factory works and workers. *DMC photo*

in so many of the car's likely competitors. On the plus side was that it was a readily available production engine that was already emissions-certified and available in sufficient quantity at reasonable cost. An early idea was to turbo-charge the engine, which would have brought power up to more competitive, if not noteworthy, levels. After high-level meetings with Citroen leadership, it was decided that DeLorean seek other powertrain options.

While these issues were being solved and finalized, the prototypes made the rounds in search of investor money and additional dealers. Sales and marketing chieftain Dick Brown spearheaded these howdy rounds, and even though the production DeLorean would differ in countless details, it looked conceptually close enough to what the final product would be to appear credible. The opening windows in the door would be of a different design and shape, as would the "gill" vents that appeared just aft of the door openings. The wheel designs were different, and the interior was vastly different. In the philosophy that the DeLorean was thought of as a "safety car," the first model prototype wore a large steering wheel with a large padded center boss, easily six-inches (15 cm) in diameter, plus a cabinwide knee bolster underneath the dash intended to prevent occupant submarining and leg injuries in the event of a hard frontal crash. Italdesign would freshen up some of the car's edges,

creases, and curves for final production. After all, the original design themes were created in the mid-1970s, and ditto the prototypes, for a car coming to market six to seven years later. So, the "suit needed pressing," you might say, and it came out fresh and ready to wear.

The search continued for a suitable powertrain and ultimately led the DeLorean contingent to Peugeot-Renault-Volvo (PRV), which produced a single overhead camshaft (SOHC), 90 degree V-6 in the appropriate size (2.4- to 3.0-liters [146.5 to 183.1 cu in]) and power ranges that seemed a likely fit for the DMC-12. Being a SOHC design layout, it was a bit more sophisticated than many of the V-6s being produced by American carmakers at the time, most of which were generally less sporty and often lower revving, all or a majority of them cast iron construction, overhead valve (OHV) designs. Also of benefit is the French engine's aluminum alloy block and cylinder heads, which reduces overall weight and improves power-to-weight ratio.

This pathway offered several advantages to the DeLorean project. The first being that the powertrain was of appropriate engine displacement and packaging size that would fit logically in the back of the car. Some mistakenly

Above: We have a chassis and now a powertrain. PRV's Douvrain 2.85-liter (173.91 cu in), all aluminum SOHC V-6 was available, affordable, came with viable transmission options, easy to certify in terms of emissions and fuel economy, fit within the confines of the DeLorean's chassis and engine bay, and put out commendable, if not scintillating, power. It was a solid and justifiable choice certainly at the time and among the other options, if not ultimately an exotic engine choice.

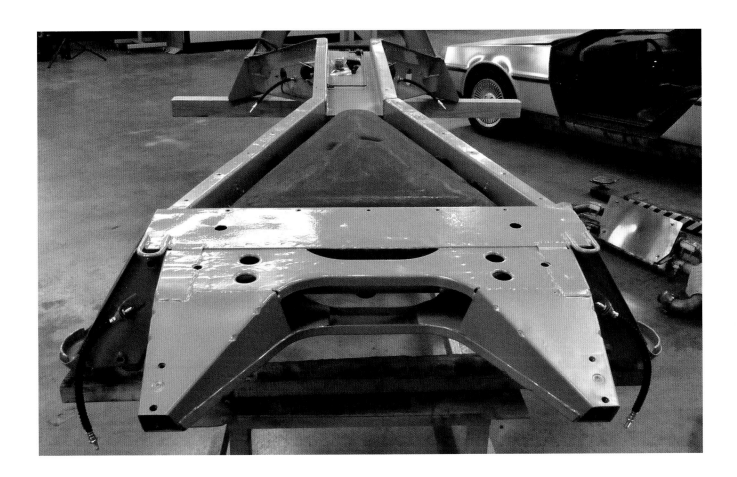

Above: A largely bare central backbone DeLorean chassis, as viewed from the front. The triangle shaped gray/black component in the front center is the fuel tank, its logical location not only in terms of packaging safety, but also as weight offset to the rear-mounted powertrain.

believe that the engine was installed in a transverse manner, but that's not true—the entire powertrain sits longitudinally, which made it rather long with engine and transmission connected as installed—more packaging issues was something no mid- or rear-engine car needs. Additionally, workable transmission offerings were available with it, meaning a five-speed manual transaxle and an automatic. Of further importance was that the engine's source was a reliable one, not a third world, backwater start-up engine builder, and could provide the engine in near any volume needed. If DMC wanted two engines, PRV could supply them—or two thousand or twenty thousand. After much research, testing, and evaluation, a 2.8-liter (170.9 cu in) spec V-6 unit would be developed for DMC use. The target horsepower rating was an estimated 135 (99 kW), which doesn't sound like much in today's parlance, but remember that when looking at it through the lens of the late 1970s and early 1980s, it seemed like enough given the marketplace. It wasn't so many years prior that the once mighty Corvette's 350 cu in (5.7 L) small-block V-8 was rated a 150 horsepower (110 kW); wheezing through a single catalytic converter, the 1982 Mustang GT's 302 V-8 was rated at 137 horsepower

(101 kW) (although with very V-8 like torque); and the Porsche 911's 2.7-liter (164.8 cu in) flat-six in North American spec was good for just 157 (110 kW). Thus, a 135 horsepower (99 kW) rating wasn't so far out of the ballpark (and this was yet without any consideration of the Renault Alpine 3.0-liter [183.1 cu in] displacement version of the PRV engine—and it was far too early to even utter the word "turbocharger"). Other than the nickname PRV, this engine is also often referred to as the Douvrain V-6, based on the location of its primary French production facility. Yet another potential sweetener in the use of the PRV V-6 is that since it was in active production, emissions and safety certified, and sold in vehicles all around Europe and in a few cases, the United States (as Volvo employed versions of the engine in several of its models), was the potential for piggybacking on the emissions and durability testing and certifications the engine had already earned in other applications. One way that DeLorean could refine, develop, and test the engine as it would appear in the DMC-12 was to prototype it in a handful of Renault Alpine A310 sport coupes, of which DMC ultimately owned four. The A310, like the DMC-12, ran the Douvrain engine, also mounted behind the rear axle line, thus making it technically rear-engined as the DeLorean would be.

So, a viable DMC-12 package was coming together, even though it yet lacked suitable chassis and construction solutions. The car needed to be production engineered and fully productionized, so that each and every component could be precisely measured, spec'd, sourced, and priced no matter if it was being produced in-house or purchased from an outside supplier.

Collins, DeLorean, and the team scoured the world for carmakers and/or engineering concerns that could and would production engineer the DMC-12. DeLorean spoke to Mercedes-Benz and to Porsche: two brands that knew how to produce specialized cars and known for quality engineering prowess. Both proved to be non-starters, as the German juggernauts were certainly capable of the job, but it would take too long and cost too much.

The search brought DMC to the considerable doorstep of Anthony Colin Bruce Chapman, the driving force, founder, inspiration, and primary brain trust behind Lotus Cars, which he founded in 1952. He was an inventor, designer, engineer, and racing team patron—and largely successful at all of them—based in England.

A tour de force automotive engineering powerhouse, he was credited for the term "add lightness," meaning not just to subtract weight from a vehicle but to engineer in lightness, which invariably makes a car faster and handle better. He had also innovated more than a few chassis concepts and designed and produced whole or parts of high-performance engines. Under his direction, Team Lotus won seven Formula One (F1) Constructors' Championships, six Formula One Drivers' Championships, and the Indianapolis 500 in the United States, between 1962 and 1978. Chapman could do the job

Above: Lotus epicenter Colin Chapman, handsomely charming in an engaging British way, was a positively brilliant design engineer. He knew how to bring a car from idea to production and how to get good power out of a small engine and improve handling and performance by keeping a watchful eye on weight. *Lotus Cars photo.* **Opposite:** No, it's not James Bond or actual on-screen Bond Girls, but several iterations of Lotus Esprit served famously in two 007 films: *The Spy Who Loved Me* and *For Your Eyes Only*. *Bonhams Auctions photo*

and was willing. It wasn't an immediate nor perfect marriage, but the foibles were smoothed out, and the two companies got together. Mr. DeLorean also offered Chapman a far more than considerable amount of money to take the job. The first and near immediate casualty of this arrangement was DMC chief engineer Bill Collins—there just wasn't enough room in the compact De-Lorean orbit for two engineering chieftains. Chapman and his team at Lotus were staying, and Collins was not.

One factor seen as both a positive and a negative in this arrangement was that Lotus's own Esprit (star, along with Roger Moore, in two James Bond movies). The mid-engined, fiberglass-bodied Esprit was also designed by Giugiaro and was not entirely dissimilar to the DMC-12 in overall size and shape and would certainly be seen as a legit competitor to it. Some predicted and/or feared potential conflicts of interest—a legitimate concern. Inasmuch as the

DeLorean's political landscape was seen as an uphill battle from the beginning (an American organization producing cars in North Ireland, with the endeavor being primarily financed by the British Government), it didn't hurt from a brownie points aspect that such a big portion of the engineering job and funds was being shared with an English company.

Lotus established a DeLorean team that would work out of the DeLorean factory in Belfast, while certain other engineers and development specialists continued on at Lotus' facilities in Hethel, Norfolk, United Kingdom. Among the many, often simultaneous engineering jobs that needed to be dealt with before too many more production and supplier decisions could be made was the need for a workable chassis solution. For this, Lotus had a viable solution in hand as close as its own production line. Colin Chapman had developed the "central spine" chassis architecture over several years and in a number of Lotus models. The spine-chassised model that most closely resembled DeLorean's overall packaging and dimension was the Esprit. Again, the previously

Above: If there's anything that gave DMC engineers, and often later owners, headaches it was the gullwing doors. Without question, one of the DMC-12's most interesting and defining features, there were problems with leakage and occasionally, doors refusing to open or close. *Italdesign photo*

Above: *MotorTrend* Editor in Chief C. Van Tune once proclaimed that "there are no bad car photos ever taken in Europe." This photo of a DeLorean in a park near Turin, somewhat haphazardly parked in front of this elegant statue, and some metal roadblocks, with random compact cars visible in the background, still looks cool. *Italdesign photo*

envisioned ERM resin chassis notion had been set aside, and the team went to work developing a steel central spine (or backbone) chassis that would underpin the DMC-12. Made up of semi-boxed steel sections, the chassis is at its narrowest in the passenger compartment. Then, two "wishbones" of semi-boxed steel widen out front and rear, in order to accommodate subframes that will carry the suspension, powertrain, and such. Alejandro de Tomaso also experimented with central spine chassis in several race car models, plus the exotic Vallelunga and Mangusta coupes. The powertrain would be mounted far enough aft in the DeLorean's chassis to allow a bit of a package shelf deck inside the decidedly two-passenger compartment. The pros and cons of this central spine chassis layout can be debated ad infinitum, but the immediate benefits were that it was technologically feasible and would accommodate the DMC-12s passenger compartment, powertrain, and other mechanical systems. Plus, the primary Engineering arm—Lotus—had experience with it.

Above: The first prototype bodyshell for one of Lotus's all-time hallmark machines, the mid-engined Europa. The Europa, like the DMC-12, also road aboard a central spine chassis, wrapped in fiberglass body-work so light and thin you could practically see through it. *Motoring Picture Library/Alamy Stock photo*

The originally envisioned ERM body/chassis design was to incorporate an underbody that would have included the passenger compartment "tub" area that would mount the seats, console, and most everything else in the cabin. The central spine chassis didn't have any such provision, so instead, a fiberglass underbody (molded in two pieces with separate molds for each) was designed to fill this need. It used a top and a bottom mold section in order to provide the proper shape and finish to this new underbody and thus front and rear-engine and storage compartments. It was not as potentially tricky as the ERM unibody might have been, far easier to design and produce, and more than up to the job. This underbody would form the floors, front compart-ment, and rear-engine compartment area of the car, but was not to be used as a "stressed component" in the mounting of suspension or powertrain. It would also serve as a mounting bed for several of the stainless steel body panels.

Lotus was the first carmaker to viably produce central spine chassis'd automobiles; Italy's DeTomaso was another, although either's production numbers pale in comparison to any major producer.

Another immediate engineering challenge was a viable and producible mechanism to which the gullwing doors could be mounted and operated. For this, the Grumman Aerospace Corporation was involved as a technology partner. The solution was a vertically slim steel "door box" that would be mounted in the centermost section of the roof panel, just inside of the gullwing door openings. The key to making this affair work was a "cryogenically stressed" torsion bar that would act as a counterbalance spring to carry the majority of the door's weight through the up and down swings of the door. They put the "raw" bar that had been stretched and straightened into the correct size and shape into a freeze tank of liquid nitrogen (at about minus 325 degrees Fahrenheit [minus 198 degrees Celsius]) and then mechanically twisted through 10 revolutions. This action rearranged the grain and molecular structure of the metal, so that at normal temperatures, it became a spring in the twisting motion direction. It was nicknamed the Grumman "crysotwist" spring bar, which would be produced by a company called SPS Technologies.

The development and productionizing process of the DMC-12 meant the letting of myriad supplier and subcontractor arrangements and contracts, including several large and well known American companies: ACDelco was signed on to do the gauges and instrumentation clusters, and GM's Harrison Radiator Corporation subsidiary signed on for the climate systems. Goodyear was on to supply its (then) high-tech, high-performance NCT model tires. The second prototype, running a PRV V-6 and many more production spec systems and components (and styling and design touches) than the first Citroen powered machine, was being developed, built, and tested throughout much of 1978, about two years downstream of that original first prototype machine.

Even though prototype 2 advanced what the DMC-12 would look like, be made of, and become, it was far from a full-fledged nor production ready car. The late John Lamm, in his seminal book about the earliest days of DeLorean, *De Lorean: Stainless Steel Illusion*, summarized the second development car's status accordingly: "In early summer, 1978, where the car was undergoing heating and cooling [development] runs, Colin Chapman and [Lotus executive] Mike Kimberly first came to see the DMC-12 at the invitation of John DeLorean. Later, they said the car was abominable…" Much work remained.

DeLorean was said to be aiming to release the car into the marketplace and thus the public, as a 1980 model, yet too much work remained to meet this deadline, so development worked continued, and the car was smartly retargeted to appear as a 1981 model. The primary intended marketplace was North America, for which most of the production volume would be specified for, with smaller handfuls of cars built to European spec for various markets other than the United States.

The relationship between DeLorean's management team and those of Lotus was frosty from the get-go. Neither totally trusted the other and likely felt and acted like one company's existence would be nearly automatically detrimental to the other, and vice versa. Which is quite a shame, as the two companies had a lot to offer each other, and healthy partnerships are seldom built upon such feelings and actions. By this time, Lotus was still developing its new Lotus Total Technology subsidiary, with the intent of offering contract automotive R&D services. The DeLorean engineering development deal brought much (and seemingly always) needed work and funding to Lotus's doorstep.

Yet, it's easy to understand how suspicions might develop. Some Lotus employees felt that DeLorean would get more attention (resources, engineering efforts, and innovations) than its own house brand. Some in the DeLorean camp felt it would go the other direction in that Lotus would "save" the best (resources, engineering efforts, innovations, *and* people) for itself. Although this generally proved not to be the case, the relationship was a chilly one. Despite the fact that they were both highly engineering driven, Colin Chapman and John DeLorean couldn't have otherwise been two more different types of guys.

The first priority was to develop a workable, production feasible chassis by which to underpin the car. A monocoque (unibody) approach was at the time a generally tried and true design philosophy for a lightweight sports car—Porsche, among several other carmakers, employed this philosophy to great extent. But to develop such a design for DeLorean would have cost too much and taken too long. Ditto for a full tubular frame, much as Ferrari used for most of its cars at the time. But with Lotus came an obvious answer to that question, to design a central spine chassis (frame) whereupon the suspension, powertrain, and front and rear subframes could handle the engine, transaxle, and suspension mounting points and to which the passenger floor and body would be affixed. This proved to be the shortest distance between two points, and Lotus already had practical experience with it, so a central spine chassis it would be. This could now be designed around the final engine of choice, the PRV 2.8-liter (170.9 cu in) V-6, which also needed productionizing, exhaust systems, and emissions testing and certification in the DMC-12. Something else of value that Lotus also brought to the DeLorean table is lots of experience with fiberglass. Remember how the ERM composite sandwich process thought to be usefully developed for the DeLorean was ultimately estimated not to be so? Well, Lotus already had and offered its Vacuum Assisted Resin Injection (VARI) technology and production process to get the DMC-12's underthings ready for a new steel chassis and do the job for the passenger compartments, floor, front trunk, and engine bay. Somewhat like ERM, the activation of VARI for the DeLorean retained producing the structures via upper and lower haves that would have been bonded together to form a mostly singular structure. Something else that made VARI easier to adopt was that it could be formed in molds, instead of stamping dies. Upper and lower molds, each of top and

Certain comparisons between the Lotus Esprit and the DeLorean DMC-12 are reasonable, but calling the DeLorean an "American Esprit" is not.

bottom pieces, would be easier and cheaper to design and produce for the DeLorean than having to engineer the pressing dies required by ERM.

Group Lotus was officially contracted into the DeLorean engineering and productionizing process in late 1978, and although a 1981 production vehicle launch into market seemed like a long way off, there was much work to be done and not unlimited time in which to do it. John DeLorean seemed pleased overall with the arrangement, as he contrasted it with other options: "I'm convinced we got a much less expensive job [from Lotus], and a much better job than we'd have been able to contract in the United States. Possibly Porsche could have done a better job, but it would have [cost more] and taken more time."

We've not yet spoken much about suspension design and hardware—something Lotus could absolutely help with based on its experience with production sports cars and in racing. The Esprit's MacPherson strut front suspension was judged an ideal fit for the DMC-12, so it was subscribed virtually unchanged, other than for final tuning. It was convenient in that it was already on hand and fit the Esprit's central backbone chassis, which was by no means identical to the DeLorean chassis. The rear suspension from the Esprit wasn't wholly adopted, and ended up being redesigned a bit and retuned to incorporate an additional upper link. Given that owners and automotive media alike ranked the Esprit as a great driving car, this boded well for these bits' use in the DeLorean.

Comparisons between the DMC-12 and the Lotus Esprit were inevitable. Other than the use of gullwing doors vs. conventional doors and stainless steel body panels vs. fiberglass panels, the two cars square up somewhat similarly:

	Lotus Esprit	DeLorean DMC-12
WHEELBASE	96.0 IN (243.8 CM)	94.8 IN (240.8 CM)
OVERALL	167.7 IN (426.0 CM)	168.0 IN (426.7 CM)
WIDTH	73.2 IN (185.9 CM)	78.3 IN (198.9 CM)
HEIGHT	43.8 IN (111.3 CM)	44.9 IN (114.0 CM)
CURB WEIGHT	2,350 LB (1,066 KG)	2,840 LB (1,288 KG)
HORSEPOWER	140 HP (103 KW) @ 6,500 RPM	130 HP (96 KW) @ 5,500 RPM

The DeLorean was intended more of a *grand turismo*, or gentleman's grand touring sports car, with all out performance and racetrack prowess being less significant issues for the DMC-12 than they would be for a Lotus or Ferrari. As you can see, the DeLorean was generally just a pinch and an inch larger and heavier in some dimensions compared to the original first generation Esprit. The Lotus's naturally aspirated Inline four-cylinder engine was about a match to the DMC-12's V-6 powerwise, but the Esprit's lighter weight gave it a near automatic performance advantage via its more favorable weight to power ratio.

Another comment that came up upon early media reports, and those of general naysayers, is that the DMC-12 would be little more than an American Esprit. That was not fair and not true. While some basic dimensions and layout parameters are indeed similar, and the same man designed both cars, and there is definitely a fair amount of engineering underneath by Lotus, both cars possess and give off much different personalities. John DeLorean never mentioned nor marketed any racing notions for the DMC-12, yet motorsport was a decidedly fundamental aspect of Lotus' DNA. Plus, the DeLorean's stainless steel coachwork and gullwing doors give it a more distinctive personality as

Above: This fascinating prototype (on right) vs. production (left) photo tells a lot about how the detailing of the look progressed. The immediate tells on the production car is that the upper grille area and lower front fascia are more fully realized with lights and now finished in black. Note that the mirror designs are completely different, and the doors on the production car open just a smidge higher. Yet, the look and familial connection is undeniable. *DMC photo*

compared to the Lotus. So, when analyzed with any thought, the "American Lotus" notion becomes little more than a cheap shot one-liner.

In order to finalize the detail, measurements, and spec of countless pieces and parts needed to produce a DMC-12, after the early full-sized epowood-style concept, the Citroen powered running model, and the initial V-6 prototypes, a series of cars were built for countless hours and miles (kilometers) of testing and development work. For smoothing out of systemic bumps on the factory floor, a series of preproduction testing prototypes were also built. Thirty of these "pilot production cars" dubbed Dorises were built, and some of them got nicknames (Doris #4, Doris 7, Doris whatever) while out on the road or in various testing programs. According to Classic DMC President James Espey, "many of the earlier ones were cannibalized for parts on subsequent builds. Some of them had nicknames but nothing official. Pilot 9 is the earliest known survivor. 19, 20, 21 and 25 are others that managed to elude destruction." ∎

Even though the factory property had been built out and equipped in near record times, there were problems and process issues that needed to be worked out. It is great testimony to the efforts of the early band of DeLorean execs, the construction companies, and the belief in the mission. It's quite amazing that the mostly bare land went from a muddy peat bog, with two rivers that needed to be relocated, to a factory able to produce its first real production spec car, in just 28 months, including engineering, development, and certification for sale.

There were myriad production issues along the trail—so many of them falling squarely on the shoulders of the gullwing doors. Countless running and production changes and updates (something on the order of 5,000 were made throughout the car's short production life). Early doors didn't fit all that well, or stuck closed, and there were issues with the locking and window mechanisms. Meaningful quality assurance inspections and measures meant that many such foibles were addressed prior to completion and/or shipping to market. John DeLorean insisted that the cars had to be as "right as possible" before arrival at dealers, even to the extent of two factory Quality Assurance Centers were established in the United States. The doors were so fussy to build that they earned their own production space and line.

In his seminal book, *De Lorean: Stainless Steel Illusion*, the late John Lamm summarizes a big moment in DeLorean history thus: "On January 21, 1981, the first real production DeLorean rolled out of the building. Then it was a matter of the workers and managers and the car all getting to know each other, so the process could be [further] smoothed out."

There were several hundred incomplete cars, or at least inner body/chassis cars sans their stainless bodywork, built initially. These were often referred to as the "black cars." These only semi-complete cars were built in April 1981 and upon final buildout were the first DeLoreans shipped to the United States, arriving in June.

Perhaps the greater unknown, aside from the design, technology, and engineering aspects of creating a new from the tires up automobile, was what to expect of the previously unskilled workers and of the risks and impacts of

Opposite: Most people have the visual notion of a car factory being a dark, noisy, smoky, smelly place—not at John DeLorean's company, it's not. Yes, certain portions of the property were much noisier and more industrial, but the assembly areas were brightly lit, clean, safe, and generally immaculate, something that everyone in Dunmurry took great pride in. Note the nearly fully dressed chassis in the left foreground of this shot. *Alexx Michael Archive photo*

Below: It was a proud day for everyone at Dunmurry when the first production DMC-12 rolled out of the factory loading door under its own power. Here, a group of employees and execs gather for a team shot. *Trinity Mirror/Mirrorpix/Alamy Stock photo*

Cue the strains of *Impossible Dream*: countless naysayers proclaimed that building a new automobile factory from a greenfield site in wartorn Belfast, Northern Ireland, and actually producing cars simply couldn't not be done. Yet John DeLorean, a highly dedicated and motivated management team, plus hundreds of hard working local employees, got it done at least for a while.

producing anything as large and complicated as automobiles in politically and religiously war-torn Belfast. It is testimony to the original concept of establishing the plant in Belfast that workers of both religious and all political parties worked together, day in and out, side by side, with no meaningful personnel problems. The assembly workers were so pleased at having worthwhile, well-paying jobs that any of the issues that so troubled the local world outside the factory confines stayed largely below the surface, and the crew just generally got on with the work.

The workforce was certainly willing to work. Some of these folks had never held living wage jobs, and many more had often been out of work for years. DeLorean management wisely set aside plenty of space (and effort in the factory buildings) for training areas. Nothing's ever perfect, but the factory staff got lots of quality training and applied themselves accordingly—they knew that to a certain extent, the fate of the car, the company's success, as well as their future earning capability, rested upon their own shoulders. It wasn't perfect but effort was made. The political landscape that lived just outside of Dunmurry's gates was more difficult to predict or control.

The first impact of the West Belfast political turmoil affected DMC as early as the original groundbreaking ceremony. The locals committed some fire-bombing quite close to the factory, and offices and materials were destroyed, although nobody was hurt. Another impact came in a somewhat indirect manner, in that on any given day, a certain number of factory workers either needed time (or days) off to attend a mate's funeral, the latter a victim to some other violent activity in the nearby towns.

The tumultuous turf war and politically and religiously driven protests and battles (car bombings, murders, kidnappings, fires, etc.) often reached the global news level. One particular event was a pivotal hunger strike that drew international attention to IRA leader Bobby Sands, who had been jailed and went into self-imposed starvation and ultimately died in prison on May 5, 1981. West Belfast was literally a war zone between the Catholics and Protestants, and one group of rioters got close enough to the DeLorean factory property to firebomb a small wooden building within the factory grounds. This building housed the office of chief engineer Mike Losby, and thus many engineering drawings were burned and destroyed. This caused a scramble to replace the drawings and other engineering documentation. The company filed a claim with the Irish government, ultimately collecting about $800,000, which may or may not have been fair or complete compensation for the company's damages—DMC filed a further claim into the millions, which the government denied.

Needless to say, the constantly warring factors were highly disruptive to the DeLorean company's operations, although no factory workers were deeply involved, nor injured or killed—which given what was going on just outside the factory fences is somewhat amazing.

The DeLorean's construction design and engineering weren't perfect, but they were innovative and got the car from idea to production.

In between the time when the earliest production DMC-12s were being built and the car's official release to the public, the company was very busy continuing to train and improve the factory staff, sign on additional dealers (ultimately 345 dealer outlets carried the DeLorean), and raise more operating capital.

The earliest cars off the production lines suffered myriad quality issues, which had to be dealt with completely and with immediacy. Poor quality reports in the media and by the first groups of dealers and owners could sink the car and the company. Management attempted to deal with these issues in two ways. The first was to correct the issues and production processes at the factory, and the second was post-shipping to the United States at two company owned Quality Assurance Centers—one on the east coast in Bridgewater, New Jersey, the other on the opposite side of the country in Santa Ana, California. Some cars needed a few minor adjustments and just a bit of spiffing up to be ready for release to the dealer network, while others needed hundreds of hours of fettling to make right. Several factory employees were sent from Belfast not only to help with the work, but to see firsthand the issues and help with process improvements on the production lines. This helped considerably, as by mid-1981, the cars were much better.

Above: Semi-assembled chassis and underbodies were used in this state as training tools for the assembly workers. This also gives a look at what lay beneath the DMC-12's brushed steel panels. *Alexx Michael photo.*

Opposite: We and others have used the expression "war-torn" Belfast, and as you can see from this period news photo the description was unfortunately apt. Car and building bombings were daily occurrences in Northern Ireland at the time. The building destruction and murder rates were off the charts. It's no wonder that local unemployment ranged between 30 and 50 percent. *Homer Sykes/Alamy Stock photo*

Evolution

Naturally, there were many "running changes" and model evolutions that addressed some of the quality issues. These are discussed in detail in James Espey's excellent book, *The Illustrated Buyer's Guide to DeLorean Automobiles* (see Additional Reading and Resources), so we won't focus on them here. Many were under the skin, likely unknown by or invisible to dealers and buyers. Most DeLoreans were intended to be driven as sports cars and enjoyed by typical sports car drivers and buyers, so the five-speed manual transmission was the primary drivetrain choice. However, some certain percentage of the particularly North American buyership was used to and wanted an automatic transmission, which was offered as a $650 option. The earliest production cars had a "flipper door" hiding the gas filler cut into the front hood, feeding the fuel tank that was mounted in the center of the chassis. This was ultimately eliminated (at around vehicle identification number [VIN] 03200), forcing the owner to open the front hood to access the fuel cap and filler neck. The DeLorean's front trunk hood panel saw three subtly different design evolutions: the

earliest (up to approximately VIN 03200) featured the above noted external fuel filler flipper door; the next included a pair of "style lines" stamped into the metal that ran from the base of the hood nearest the windshield forward to the end of the hood at just about the interior line of each centermost headlight and no fuel filler door; and finally, a more uniformly flat hood panel that embodied neither the filler door nor the stamped style lines, although this late production piece included a cast metal *DeLorean* logotype emblem.

Initially, all of the cars were produced with an all-black interior—carpeting, dashboard, knee production padding below the dash, the Bridge of Weir leather trimmed seats, everything inside was black. Some magazine journalists, dealers, and owners complained that this made the DMC-12's interior a bit cave-like, so a combination gray and black interior was offered, which definitely lightened and brightened up the cabin. There was also some call for

Above: This is a great look at four distinct phases of DeLorean production: fully equipped chassis moving toward the body and chassis mating process (top left); interior and glass fitting (top right), which also gives a good look at the urethane casting of the front fascia with vertical mounting and stiffening beams integral to the pressing; final finishing (lower left) with all glass installed and the seats wrapped in plastic, while the front trunk area has not yet been trimmed or equipped; and finally, a mostly complete example (lower right). *Alexx Michael Archive photo*

Above: A beautifully restored DMC-12 with the "gray" interior. Scottish Bridge of Weir leather was an appropriate choice for the DeLorean, and the gray tones really lightened and brightened up the cabin. Note that the carpeting is not black, in this case just merely black floormats and the cast in DMC logo in the rocker plate.

a caramel/butterscotch tan trimmed cabin (so popular in most Italian sports cars of the time, such as Ferrari and Maserati), which was prototyped, mocked up, and used on a pair of specially built custom examples, but which did not become a regular Production Option (RPO).

Let's also remember that the DeLorean ran a "staggered" wheel and tire fitment with 14x6-inch (36x15 cm) wheels in front and 15x8-inch (38x20 cm) cast alloys in back to mount larger and wider rear tires to better balance the car's handling in light of its rearward weight distribution. Plus, early production cars, up to about VIN 01883, were built with these wheels painted a darker "graphite" gray color. After VIN 01883, examples were painted a lighter, brighter silver. There were also minor design evolutions to the rear deck louvers and also the center console inside. ■

The automotive enthusiast media magazines reported heavily and constantly about the DeLorean's development and its reality as a car. This generally came in three waves: when the car was first announced and the non-running and running models and prototypes were revealed to the public; as the result of a "media junket" event hosted by the company where in magazine editors and photographers were invited to Dunmurry to spend time with John DeLorean and other executives, see the factory and production lines, and drive a variety of early pilot production models; and finally, when production examples arrived in the United States and were loaned to the media for extensive road testing and performance evaluation. As you might expect, opinions and conclusions varied greatly depending upon the individual writer(s) and attitudes of the outlet. Most of the magazine writers agreed that building a new company, brand, and automobile in just a few years' time was a remarkable achievement. The car's styling and design earned generally warm reception and praise, although some felt the car was underpowered and didn't perform as well as anticipated, with 0–60 miles per hour (0–97 kph) times of around 10 seconds. The cabin drew generally good comment for being roomy, comfortable, and handsome.

Here's what they wrote:

The chips are down, the waiting is over, and now the game begins. John Zachary DeLorean against the odds. John DeLorean as the game-but-vulnerable champion of the all-American Horatio Alger ethic. The last stand of the individual entrepreneur in a business world populated by faceless conglomerate giants.
— Tony Swan, *Car and Driver*

The prospective DeLorean buyer isn't a bargain hunter; he's a person who wants the latest—be it car, stereo, or cowboy hat— because it satisfies his ego and makes a statement to the rest of the world. I expect the DeLorean will sell quite well, at least in its

"DeLorean is not a hard-edged answer to the 911 Porsche, nor is it another fatuous Corvette-clone. And while it stretches the established sports-car performance envelope not an iota, this car is at least happy with itself."
—Don Sherman,
Car and Driver

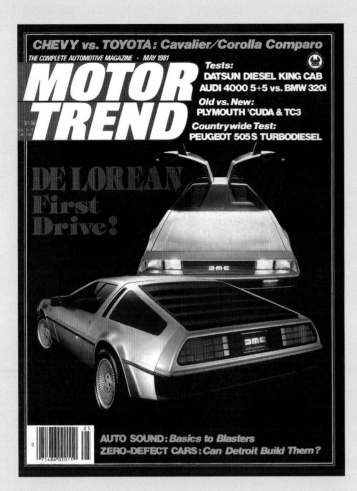

Left: It would take some time and effort to collect a copy of every magazine that put a DeLorean on its cover, particularly in 1981 as everyone hungered for media driving impressions and actual performance testing. **Right:** Note the date of this *Car and Driver* magazine photo—July 1977. This is the first running model/prototype with the four-cylinder Citroen engine. Note the dual tipped, single center exhaust outlet and the non-production side windows.

first year. The secret of long-term success though, is the company's ability to bring out a second generation car, such as the 4-door sedan already being talked about. It's going to be a long arduous process, and there are many people, particularly in Detroit, who are hoping John DeLorean will fall flat on his face. On the other hand, lots of people in Northern Ireland, and lots of taxpayers in Great Britain, who put millions of pounds in loans and grants, are rooting for a DeLorean victory. Only time will tell.
— Thomas L. Bryant, *Road & Track*

Lovers of high performance should shop elsewhere, in particular at their Porsche dealers. But for a high content, high quality, highly unique profile piece that'll get you there in comfort and enviable style, John Z's dream car looks like something of a bargain.
— *MotorTrend* ∎

5: TRIBULATIONS AND TRIALS

IT'S A SHAME THAT TOO MUCH OF THE DELOREAN STORY IS IDENTIFIED AND RE-MEMBERED BY A DRUG TRAFFICKING TRIAL.

Nobody ever did or will accuse John DeLorean of having a lack of confidence: either in himself, his company, or his stainless steel dream machine.

Nor will many people accuse him of out-and-out *intentionally lying* about his projections for the production and sales of his car and DMC's various financial pictures. Did he *exaggerate* those numbers or adjust them to suit the need or audience? Seemingly often.

Understanding exactly the financial perils that plagued DeLorean Motor Cars from its near beginning would take rooms full of paperwork, documents, and financial plans, plus a battalion of highly qualified forensic accounts to fully comprehend and summarize.

To begin, despite a big pile of loans, grants, and loan guarantees provided by the British government, the company was always "behind the cash 8 ball." When a new business of this magnitude is founded, its income is virtually nil, and start-up expenditures are fast and furious. Building an executive management team, simultaneously hiring highly qualified and experienced leadership, on both sides of the Atlantic, is an immediate and constant drain of cash, and actual income seems lightyears away. Even though the Belfast property was acquired for virtually nothing, preparing the site for automotive production use and building a factory virtually from the ground up drains cash at an amazing rate—never mind designing and engineering a new exotic car from square one and equipping a factory to produce it.

At a meeting with investors, he would quote a certain number of units produced per year, and in a media interview that number would vary—a lot (see above). Then, he would tell dealers to expect a volume of such and such, again with little correlation to previously announced, published, or planned upon numbers. Although, he remained consistent in his praise of the car, his management team, factory workers, and dealers.

Early sales failed to meet expectations, much of which was largely driven by a general economic downturn, particularly in terms of the housing and car markets. Inflation was running high, as were general levels of interest rates, not to mention that the price levels of the car had increased precipitously. When John DeLorean began discussing his notions of an ethical sports car that would be reasonable to buy and made to last, pricing estimates were in the $12,000 range—hence the model name DMC-12—which wasn't reasonable nor sustain-

Opposite top: Both the car and the man DeLorean were very much part of the Dream that the company was selling. It is impressive that the company ultimately enlisted the commitment and cash investment of 345 dealers to sell the single model only DeLorean brand—certain to splash up the showroom floor of any Cadillac, Buick, or truck dealership. Unfortunately, the dream was over all too soon. **Opposite bottom:** What is today the sprawling, palatial Trump National Golf Course Bedminster Resort in New Jersey once was the forested acreage and commanding home of the Cristina and John DeLorean family. *Madeleine Jettre/Alamy Stock Photo*

Your eyes skim the sleek, sensuous stainless steel body, and all your senses tell you, "I've got to have it!"

The counterbalanced gull-wing doors rise effortlessly, beckoning you inside.

The soft leather seat in the cockpit fits you like it was made for your body.

You turn the key. The light alloy V-6 comes to life instantly.

The De Lorean. Surely one of the most awaited automobiles in automotive history.

It all began with one man's vision of the perfect personal luxury car. Built for long life, it employs the latest space-age materials.

Of course, everyone stares as you drive by. Sure, they're a little envious. That's expected. After all, you're the one Living The Dream.

Start living it today at a dealer near you.

THE DE LOREAN. LIVE THE DREAM.

A dealer commitment as unique as the car itself. There are 345 De Lorean dealers located throughout the United States. Each one is a stockholder in the De Lorean Motor Company. This commitment results in a unique relationship which will provide De Lorean owners with a superb standard of service.

For the dealer nearest you, call toll free 800-447-4700, in Ill., 800-322-4400. **DMC**

able once the stainless steel body panels, gullwing doors, and leather trimmed cabins became parts of the plan. By the time the North American window stickers were being printed, the base price had grown to $25,000, with most 1981 examples beating a bottom line manufacturer's suggested retail price (MSRP) of $26,500 to $27,500. Additionally, many potential customers (and media members) used to the torque, quick acceleration, and power of their Corvettes, muscle cars, and other sports cars, labeled the DeLorean as too slow for such an exotic car. The car's earliest quality foibles didn't help either.

Dealers were committing to decreasing orders of cars, and the lots at the factory were filling up with unsold cars. Initial demand in America for the car was strong, many dealers asking over (and often getting) sticker prices, but once the initial fury calmed a bit, sales and demand cooled, reducing sales and dealer orders.

All of this led to money problems at the company. There was widespread speculation that John DeLorean was taking more money out of the company than his compensation structure allowed for. A few senior executives accused him of out-and-out embezzlement. One, in a media interview, called John a "ten percenter," meaning that for every dollar he brought into the company via investment, he would rake off ten percent for himself, feeling he was so entitled because he brought the money in and the fact that his name was on the car and the side of the factory building. There was also accusation that DeLorean had colluded with Colin Chapman in washing funds between the two companies through Panama, although it existed primarily as a Post Office Box in Geneva (see below).

One further gemstone evidencing that John DeLorean could spend money he may or may not have had came in the form of a palatial colonial mansion, sitting on approximately 500 acres (2 square kilometers [km2]) of lush rambling countryside in Bedminster, New Jersey, that he purchased as a present for himself, wife Cristina, and his children as their home away from Manhattan. As his business and personal financial situation was impacted by all manner of circumstance, including various bankruptcies and restructuring efforts, this magnificent mansion was ultimately sold to one Donald J. Trump and has been expanded, remodeled, and reborn as the Trump National Bedminster Golf Resort.

Additionally, John DeLorean remained steadfastly resolute that the British government didn't remain true to its funding commitments. He also asked for additional funding to shore up the company's cash position and invest in future product and process improvements in Belfast. He cited the fact that the original agreements were cast under British Labor Party rule and subsequent leadership changes resulted in shifting sands in terms of overall support of the greater DeLorean investment.

He was no fan of prime minister Margaret Thatcher, often accused of taking anti-business positions on many issues, and John was convinced she was out to undermine and bankrupt the company in hopes of recovering England's investment in the project.

Above: John DeLorean was convinced from the beginning that soon-to-take-office Prime Minister Margaret Thatcher didn't like nor support the British financing deal of the entire DeLorean Motor Cars Ltd. enterprise and once in power set out to dismantle it. This occasion appears to be a particularly boozy fundraiser. *Mike Abrahams/Alamy Stock photo*

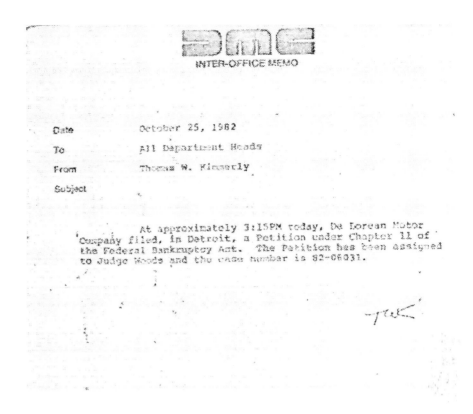

DMG
INTER-OFFICE MEMO

Date   October 25, 1982

To   All Department Heads

From   Thomas W. Kimmerly

Subject

At approximately 3:15PM today, De Lorean Motor Company filed, in Detroit, a Petition under Chapter 11 of the Federal Bankruptcy Act. The Petition has been assigned to Judge Woods and the case number is 82-06031.

October 25, 1982, was the most visible beginning of the end for the DeLorean Motor Cars story.

At this point, John DeLorean had to refocus his attentions not so much into evolving the car or developing new models, but into raising money to save the company—an activity for which he vocally claimed his disdain. The company had dialed back production and plant worker shifts to minimal levels, literally just enough to keep the proverbial lights on. John searched for financial saviors anywhere he could find them—one which would soon become infamous—from private investor sources to merger or takeover prospects. It had become a desperate rescue mission of his dream.

As bad as this quagmire of problems seemed, unfortunately, *the worst was yet to come.*

It was a simple interoffice memo–style notice, typed on a standard copier sized piece of paper, dated October 25, 1982, from company executive Thomas Kimmerly:

"At approximately 3:15 today, the DeLorean Motor Company filed, in Detroit, a Petition under Chapter 11 of the Federal Bankruptcy Act. The petition has been assigned to Judge Woods, and the case number is 82-06031."

There were several types of bankruptcy filings under US law, and Chapter 11 is the most onerous and final among them: dissolution. This single page notification was posted to the front door of the Irvine, California, company Quality Center, and thus began the expunction of the company's debts and the liquidation of assets against those debts to the extent possible. Similar notifications were soon posted at the employee and office gates in Dunmurry and New York. In so many words, the company would cease production and sales operations, be dismantled piece by piece, and sold for scrap. DMC Belfast locked its literal and metaphorical doors for good in February of 1983.

This touched off an avalanche of accusations and finger pointing, some of it aimed at the car itself and much of the rest at John DeLorean. The rumor and inuendo network became a tornado of stories about ill-gotten gains, embezzlement, dubious financial management, and a paginated litany of every mistake John and everyone else at the company made every step along the way. The DeLorean Dream had become an irreconcilable nightmare, dead all too soon after its arrival. According to today's Classic DMC parts, accessories, and restoration company in Humble, Texas, a total of 8,975 DMC-12s were produced for the 1981, 1982, and (very abbreviated) 1983 model years.

Naturally, the factory workers were grievously disappointed, having had so much faith in car, man, and company as being the keys to a good life for them and their families. Predictably, the TV news cameras set up in the company parking lots and interview one disgruntled employee after another. They were uniform and resolute in the disdain for the man they'd staked their working lives and futures on, although some still spoke highly of him. This is understandable, as they were all still shell shocked at watching John DeLorean being arrested on October 19, 1982, in a Los Angeles International Sheraton Airport Hotel (room 501) by the FBI and DEA for a drug smuggling scheme.

This historic element of the latter DeLorean nightmare had begun sometime earlier, when he confided to a neighbor named James Hoffman that he was in desperate need of major funding to save his company. After many such conversations, Hoffman ultimately came across with "a way to help" DeLorean save his business. Hoffman, other than just being a "friendly neighbor willing to help" was in fact a big-game, many times convicted drug trafficker, acting as a government informant endeavoring to curry favor and leniency with the FBI and DEA if he could help them "land a big fish," meaning to catch and convict a widely known, public figure in a drug financing and resale scam.

There were many government and otherwise players in the scam deal, but principle among them were Benedict Tisa, a senior FBI agent acting as a decidedly crooked banker who could facilitate a major cocaine resale deal requiring a relatively small investment on DeLorean's behalf that could net him as much as $5 million in cash, plus the connections to borrow another $50 or so million dollars to save his company. Tisa met with DeLorean at a bank in San Carlos, California, on September 8, 1982, just weeks before the bankruptcy filing, to help sell the ruse.

The LA bust itself—videotaped live at the LAX Sheraton La Riena (now Gateway) Hotel, room 501, on October 19, 1982—was a chilling spectacle. Front and center are John DeLorean himself, resplendent in his gray mane of hair and tailored bell-bottom dress slacks, and a small gathering of business and casually dressed guys in what appears to be a somewhat average business meeting. A suitcase is flipped open exposing what looks to be something like 34 kilos (75 pounds) of raw cocaine. DeLorean unfortunately, and a bit too enthusiastically, says it "looks as good as gold" and the guys break out the

The entire DMC property in Dunmurry exhibited a welcoming and immaculate, campuslike quality.

Right: The DeLorean facilities at Dunmurry were designed, built, and maintained to the very highest standards. John and his team insisted that anyone coming to visit, seek employment, or do business with the company be decidedly impressed that they were dealing with a solid, well-funded organization. All too soon this beautiful glass entry plaza will be locked and shuttered for good. *DMC photo*

champagne and begin toasting a "successful transaction and future business dealings" at which time FBI agent Jerry West (not related to LA Laker basketball coach of the same name) walks into the room and asks John to stand up, cuffs, formally arrests him, and reads him his Miranda rights. Cristina and the children were still in New York at the time and immediately flew to Los Angeles, buttonholed by the TV news cameras upon her arrival saying that "I know nothing yet of what happened; I just arrived, and came here in support of my husband. I know nothing," which was believed to be true. She of course knew that her husband was working feverishly to raise capital to save the company and thus the family livelihood and home, yet never dreamed that his efforts had devolved into or near such highly illegal activities.

The video recordings of the actual sting and arrest at the hotel, which were supposed to be used only by the FBI to enact their court case against DeLorean, somehow ended up in the hands of *Hustler* magazine publisher Larry Flynt who leaked (or more likely sold) them to CBS news, which immediately aired them publicly, right away bringing up accusations leading to a "made for televisions sting operation."

Claiming victimization and entrapment, if DeLorean was truly innocent and ignorant of the entire process being an illicit drug deal, you may wonder why he attended such a meeting in the first place and why would he look at the drugs as if it were a suitcase full of diamonds, and proclaim it to be "good as gold," and then thank his newfound "business associates" and begin proposing toasts.

There were at least two reasons. One being blind desperation. At this point, he was driven to the willingness to do nearly anything to (in his mind) save his dream car, company, and family. That's not a justification, but recall that this was a man who wasn't accustomed to losing, with few failures in his professional past. He was a winner's winner, and with the conviction deep in his heart that given the time, opportunity, and a big pile of cash, he could resolve the company out of its problems.

Once that suitcase was opened, why didn't he simply jump up and run out of the room, leaving the entire drug mess behind him? Beyond that was another more frightening reality. He feared for the lives of his family, and indeed himself, having received what he believed to be credible death threats if he didn't go through with the deal. Up until the moment Agent West walked into the room and flashed his FBI credentials, he legitimately felt he was dealing with dangerous drug cartels that had not only the reach to instantly make him rich, but moreover, harm or kill him and his family if the deal went south.

As DeLorean Motor Company, Ltd., made the deathwalk into dissolutional bankruptcy and its namesake John DeLorean, went to jail, awaiting trial, he and the family would ultimately move in with Cristina's parents during the trial process itself. Newsreel footage of a sleep deprived DeLorean being schlepped from holding facilities to courtrooms, handcuffed in a prisoner's jumpsuit, seemed surreal at best.

Needless to say, the drug bust scandal was world news and made more newspaper and magazine front pages than did even the world's most famous rockstars, political figures, and British Royal weddings. DeLorean staff and factory workers watched the TV news coverage in utter disbelief, as there he was persecuted and their dream jobs and future went up in metaphorical flames.

The late John Lamm, award winning *MotorTrend* and *Road & Track* magazines automotive journalist and photographer at the time said: "I've ridden with him through London in a chauffeured Rolls-Royce to buy a topcoat at Burberry's . . . and when there wasn't news film to provide the images, I tried to imagine him sitting in a jail cell on Terminal Island [a holding prison facility in San Pedro / Long Beach, California]. What was he doing, what was he thinking? I couldn't bring the image into focus. That [holding cell] was simply too far away from the Cannaught Hotel, too far from the Fifth Avenue apartment, too far from the office on 43rd Avenue."

As he awaited trial, the clearly rudderless DeLorean had nothing but time on his hands to think, contemplate his life, and roll over, again and again, in his mind, what went wrong, and of course to contemplate what sort of life he would have should he be acquitted—or convicted. Never previously portrayed as a religious man, he discovered deep faith, becoming what we'd now call "born again" into Christianity, putting his life, business, and his faith in the hands of Higher Powers. From that point on, he never appeared in court without a large, leatherbound Bible in hand—some quipped that this was a prop, yet DeLorean could recall and quote from memory many Biblical passages by scripture name or number. For the rest of his life, he was known as a devout Christian. That was something he would later acknowledge as the primary tenet in his life that got him through prison life as he awaited trial, which didn't begin until April 18, 1984, in California Superior Court in Los Angeles, under the experienced eye of Judge Robert Takasugi, with James P. Walsh Jr. and Robert Parry as lead prosecutors in the government's case.

Naturally, a lot of high-powered lawyers and law firms vied for the chance to defend DeLorean in this extremely high-profile trial. DeLorean ultimately—and wisely—settling on thoughtful veteran and highly strategic litigator Howard Weitzman as lead counsel. Weitzman was a well-known and widely respected Los Angeles attorney and educator, not known for being a flashy type "celebrity lawyer" (although he represented many celebrity-type clients). Sharing primary responsibilities with Weitzman in John DeLorean's defense was co-counsel Don Re, both backed up by the defense team's "secret weapon," attorney Mona Soo Hoo. No mere law clerk or legal assistant, Ms. Hoo acted primarily in a research capacity to help systematically remove bricks and mortar from the foundation of the prosecution's case against DeLorean. With previous experience as a county prosecutor, she'd gone freelance in pursuit of a deeper career in criminal law. John DeLorean credits her diligence, hard work, and intelligence—liberally and often—in making the defense effort a success and helping "reverse prove" how the FBI and DEA and known drug traffickers conspiratorially conspired to set DeLorean up for a big fall.

Weitzman and his small but powerful team of lawyers and researchers put in the work during DeLorean's four-month trial, digging deep into the government's tactics, methodology, and documentation, systematically poking holes into the FBI and DEA's processes and procedures. It was proven that reports and documentation were altered, manufactured, or "lost," and that the pivotal hotel room sting was highly manufactured and manipulated to ensure that DeLorean was trapped, and that several of the government agents involved had very personal and selfish career motivations for snaring and convicting such a highly visible personality such like DeLorean. Weitzman's team's research was tireless and immaculate, yet the government was cocksure it couldn't lose—after all, they had John DeLorean on so many hours of video and audio tape playing into the hands of the high stakes drug deal. It is interesting that the defense only elected to call two witnesses on John's behalf, they being DEA agent Jerry Scotti and one of John DeLorean's secretaries, Carol Winkler, whom he also credits for her poised, detailed testimony.

Ask any experienced litigator the odds of any case going any direction once in the hands of the jury, and they'll tell you that any prediction of the outcome, no matter how well reasoned, was still little better than a guess or spinning an out of balance roulette wheel. Despite the many missteps John DeLorean made along the trail of the government's setting up of the "deal," the jury required less than half a day to deliberate and reach a unanimous verdict. As scripted in John's autobiography *DeLorean*:

"The Court is in receipt of Jury Note Number One dated this date, August 16, 1984, signed by the foreperson of the jury indicating that a unanimous verdict has been reached. Mr. Foreperson, is that correct?"

"That's correct your Honor."

"Please present the written verdict to our bailiff . . . Ms. Clerk, please read the verdict."

"The verdict reads, "United States of America versus John Z. DeLorean. We the jury in the above-entitled case find the defendant John Z. DeLorean not guilt[y] as charged in Count One, not guilty as charged in Count Two, not guilty as charged in Count Three, not guilty as charged in Count Five, not guilty as charged in Count Six, not guilt[y] as charged in Count Seven, not guilty as charged in Count Eight, and not guilty as charged in Count Nine of the indictment."

The Bailiff called for quiet in the courtroom, and the judge asked for a live polling of the jurors. The acquittal was unanimous—*Not Guilty*.

John DeLorean wasn't simply a guy who made mistakes and possibly intended to do bad things, yet instead a man with an FBI/DEA target intentionally pinned to his back, set up to make his accusers famous in the eyes of law enforcement in the new Reagan era war on drugs.

Opposite top: Luckily, or brilliantly, John DeLorean selected Los Angeles standout attorney Howard Weitzman to lead his defense team at the LA Superior Court. DeLorean stood a head above him physically, but not metaphorically, having deep respect for counselor Weitzman's style, methodology, and tenacity. *MediaPunch Inc/Alamy Stock photo.* **Opposite bottom:** NOT GUILTY can be read over the faces of daughter Kathryn DeLorean (white suit, arms raised), Cristina and John DeLorean, and co-council Mona Soo Hoo gripping John's left hand just over Kat's raised left arm. *MediaPunch Inc/Alamy Stock photo*

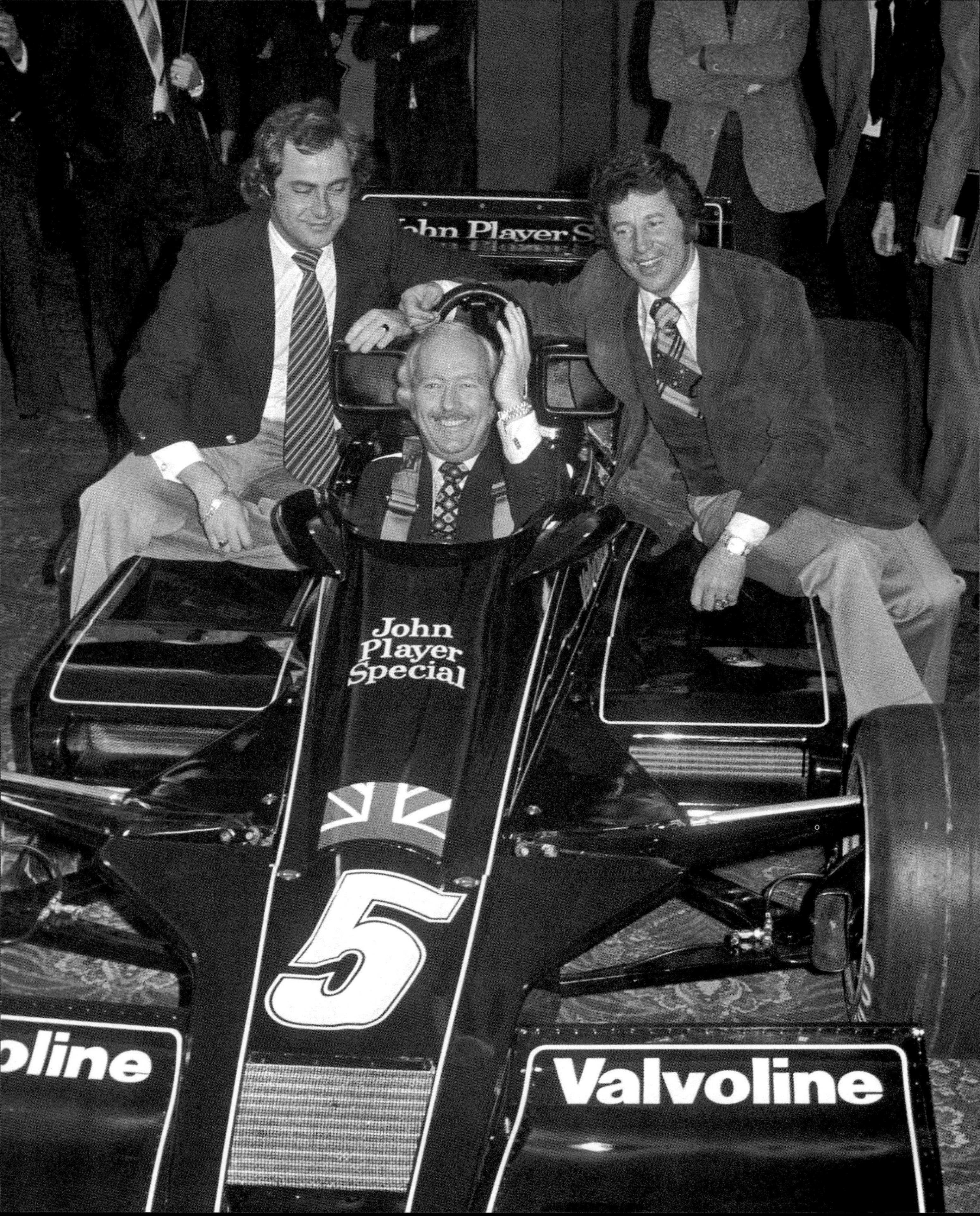
John Player S
John Player Special
5
oline
Valvoline

Even though John DeLorean and ultimately Colin Chapman were both brought to task in two major, but separate, criminal trials, both were acquitted, which wasn't enough to save them from being tarred with scandal, and sealing DMC's fate for good.

Once dismissed from the courtroom on August 16, 1984, a free man, John, his wife, and legal team all gathered on the courthouse steps to address the anxious media. DeLorean precipitously thanked "the Lord" and his legal team for freeing and saving him. He somehow looked years younger, lighter, and much more his old self, if perhaps a bit more humble.

He credited Cristina for being in court every day, literally and metaphorically standing by his side throughout the entire ordeal. What he did not know is after the several year roller coaster of leaving GM, founding the company, crisscrossing the world in search of capital, and the people, places, and means to build his company and cars, plus of course countless business, personal, and financial mistakes, the fall and the trial, she was completely "done." She had met and fallen in love with another man, and only a few days after the trial's conclusion would tell him she was leaving and divorcing him to marry television and movie industry executive Anthony Thomopoulos with whom she would have two more children. John would also sadly file personal bankruptcy and lose most of his assets, homes, and property.

And the Other Big Court Case

As if to further muddy similar waters, or add insult to injury, there was another legal tiger chasing John DeLorean around his cage about the same time as the whole drug trafficking affair: *Car and Driver* summarized it accordingly:

It was discovered that some of the company [DMC's] investment money, about $17 million assumed to have gone to Lotus, was missing. Suspicion centered around "GPD," General Product Development, a Swiss company [existing only of paperwork, and a PO box in Geneva] that was incorporated in Panama City. On paper, DeLorean [DMC] paid GPD for the development and engineering of the DMC-12, and that company subcontracted Lotus. Only Lotus appears to have never received any notable sum from GPD; sure, money flowed in directly from DeLorean Motor Company, but almost nothing from GPD. In late 1982, soon after the missing funds were called into question, Lotus's founder and head man Colin Chapman—rumored to be one of the few people next to DeLorean who truly knew what GPD's game was—died.

Interest in GPD was likely spurred after DMC's [1982] receivership and bankruptcy filings, and it really stemmed from the source of the absent money. Raised years earlier for a "research partnership" brokered by the financial firm Oppenheimer and Company, this money was dumped into a DeLorean subsidiary, the DeLorean Research Limited Partnership, and earmarked for research and development. Under contemporary tax laws, these investments could be written off; so, when the money appeared to have vanished, the IRS and its British equivalent came knocking. These inquiries eventually led to John Z. DeLorean's indictment in 1985 on 15 federal charges of fraud, racketeering, wire fraud, and more.

In spite of bad circumstance, bad dealings, and/or bad luck, DeLorean also dodged this bullet:

Almost amazingly, DeLorean successfully used an entrapment defense in his drug trial and was found not guilty.

Perhaps more amazingly, he also beat the fraud rap, even though it wasn't entirely clear where $17.75 million in investors' money had gone. Prosecutors alleged that more than $8 million of GPD cash was used by DeLorean himself to pay off loans he took out to purchase a snow-machine manufacturer in Utah—one of his many side projects that irked other DMC executives—while another half a million was simply used for personal purposes. Almost nothing had made its way to Lotus or to any actual R&D. Even DeLorean's lawyer said at the time that his client "was lucky to be acquitted in the fraud case in Detroit.

John DeLorean called the entire affair "poppycock," testifying that the R&D funds were properly channeled back into the car production development process. And apparently, again, the courts agreed.

Back in Belfast

During the two years of John DeLorean's temporary incarceration pending trial, and the trial itself, the courts and the British government were systematically dismantling DMC. Auditors combed the books for mishandled money. Crews dealt with all of the remaining finished and unfinished 1982 and 1983 DMC-12s and liquidated every tool and piece of equipment or furniture to be found at Dunmurry. It was a tragic legal, financial, and procedural autopsy.

DeLorean dealers with remaining paid for inventory couldn't seem to dump the cars quickly enough, often resorting to tasteless marketing means to do so: newspapers were rife with advertisements about how DeLoreans "Go better with Coke[caine]," riffing on then current soft drink television commercials, sometimes offering DeLoreans with their trunks filled with free cases of Coca-Cola, or how well the cars tracked on highways with "white lines" painted down the middle, mocking the visual of the cars sniffing metaphoric "lines of cocaine." Cars that were priced well above sticker just a year previous were

Opposite: As unsold DMC-12s filled finished inventory lots at Dunmurry, the company bled cash it really didn't have. It's highly likely that many of these cars ended up the property of Consolidated International as part of the final assets liquidation. *Alexx Michael Archive photo*

Building the cars obviously wasn't DMC's problem, it's that they weren't selling fast enough to keep the company machine moving and solvent.

DE LOREAN MOTOR CARS OF AMERICA
Division of DeLorean Motor Company

MODEL	BODY TYPE	PORT OF ENTRY	METHOD OF TRANSPORTATION
DELOREAN	2-DOOR	LONG BEACH, CA.	TRUCK

INTERIOR	VEHICLE IDENTIFICATION NO.	ENGINE NO.	MODEL YEAR
GRAY	SCEDT26T3DD016266	009556	1983

MANUFACTURERS SUGGESTED RETAIL PRICE ▶ $ 32,833.90

STANDARD FEATURES

- Stainless Steel Body Panels
- Counter Balanced Gull-Wing Doors
- 4-Wheel Independent Suspension
- Rack & Pinion Steering
- Electronic Ignition System
- Body Side Molding
- Tinted Windows
- Intermittent Windshield Wipers
- Epoxy Coated Corrosion Resistant Frame
- Dual Braking System
- Halogen Headlamps
- Engine/Luggage Compartment Lights
- Interior Hood & Engine Compartment Release

REAR MOUNTED 174 CID OHC V6 ENGINE	STD
5-SPEED MANUAL TRANSMISSION	STD
BOSCH K-JETRONIC FUEL INJECTION	STD
POWER ASSISTED 4-WHEEL DISC BRAKES	STD
AIR CONDITIONING	STD
AM/FM STEREO RADIO W/CASSETTE	STD
ELECTRONIC POWER ANTENNA	STD
POWER WINDOWS	STD
CENTRAL DOOR LOCKING SYSTEM	STD
MANUAL TILT & TELESCOPIC STEERING COLUMN	STD
DUAL ELECTRIC REMOTE SIDE VIEW MIRRORS	STD
CAST LIGHT-ALLOY WHEELS	STD
GOODYEAR NCT STEEL BELTED RADIAL TIRES	STD
ELECTRIC REAR WINDOW DEFOGGER	STD
DIGITAL CLOCK	STD
ELECTRIC TACHOMETER	STD
BOSCH LAMBDA EMISSION CONTROL	STD
U.S. PROCESSING CHARGES	$ 600.00

OPTIONAL EQUIPMENT
NONE

DESTINATION CHARGES	$ 575.00

*GASOLINE, LICENSE AND TITLE FEES, STATE AND LOCAL TAXES ARE NOT INCLUDED IN THE MANUFACTURER'S SUGGESTED RETAIL PRICE.

TOTAL SUGGESTED RETAIL PRICE ▶	$ 34,008.90

⊕EPA FUEL ECONOMY RATING

MODEL:

ESTIMATED MPG FOR COMPARISONS

1983 DELOREAN, 174 CID ENGINE, 6 CYLINDERS, 5-SPEED MANUAL TRANSMISSION, MECHANICAL FUEL INJECTION, CATALYST EQUIPPED, FEED BACK FUEL SYSTEM.

OTHER

TWO SEATER

MODELS

THE **ESTIMATED** MILEAGE FOR THIS MODEL, 21 , IS TO BE USED TO **COMPARE** CARS OF THIS MODEL WITH OTHER CARS. YOUR OWN MILEAGE MAY BE POORER DEPENDING UPON OPTIONS, DRIVING CONDITIONS, YOUR DRIVING HABITS, AND YOUR CAR'S OPERATING CONDITIONS

THE **ESTIMATED MPG** NUMBERS FOR OTHER SIMILAR SIZED CARS RANGE FROM 10 TO 29 MPG (AS OF SEPT. 30, 1981). BY COMPARISON, THE **ESTIMATED MPG** OF THIS VEHICLE IS 21 . USE THESE NUMBERS TO COMPARE DIFFERENT MODELS. CONSULT THE **GAS MILEAGE GUIDE** FOR FURTHER INFORMATION.

ANNUAL FUEL COST, $ 1178 BASED ON 21 MPG, 15,000 MILES PER YEAR, $1.65 /GALLON.

ASK THE DEALER FOR THE **FREE** 1982 GAS MILEAGE GUIDE TO COMPARE THE ESTIMATED MPG OF OTHER CARS. IT WILL TELL YOU HOW TO USE THESE NUMBERS.

now deeply discounted, infuriating owners who had paid the usurious premium prices. Late night talk show hosts had their way with the entire fiasco, the jokes rampant and tasteless to those who loved their cars and respected their namesake creator.

A major move in disposing of inventory still on the company's books (in other words, not yet sold to, paid for, or in the hands of dealers, who were essentially free to do as they wished with the leftover cars on their lots) was a massive disposition sale of leftover cars and significantly, repair and service inventory parts to an Ohio wholesaler called Consolidated International. What was Consolidated at the time has now become the parent company of today's Big Lots discount retailer—the business model then was much as it is now—to acquire the inventory of bankrupt companies and resell it at bargain prices for profit.

Consolidated had no experience in the automotive space at this large, or public, a scale, yet quickly established itself as an aggressive seller with something to interest enterprising dealers that recognized that the DeLorean cars still had value and interest to consumers. They marketed the cars heavily and aggressively to dealers across the country and deep discounts, with warranty backing, and attractive seller-to-dealer financing packages. The cars were brand new from the factory, carrying window stickers in the $34,000 range, and Consolidated offered them to dealers at around $21,000 apiece. And this was for remaining primarily 1983 models, the most developed and theoretically highest quality (and last) DMC-12s built. Naturally, the car buying public was still a bit shell shocked over the whole drug trial fiasco and the company's financial meltdown, but it turned out there was residual demand for the cars, especially at the potential of deeply discounted prices. The DeLorean cars were marketed as The Vanishing Breed—compellingly sad but true.

Consolidated had no experience or mechanism for dealing with crateloads of service and repair parts, not to mention piles of production parts such as body panels, glass, powertrains, wheels, seats, and everything else required to produce new cars. Rather than set up a comprehensive, yet cumbersome, parts distribution business, Consolidated sold all of this (and considerable rights to the company's name and other assets) to a company in Texas that essentially became the new DeLorean Motor Company, adopting the DMC name (see Chapter 7).

By the end of 1985, John DeLorean was broke, out of work, single again, and living in a modest apartment in New Jersey, instead of ranches, vacation homes, palatial estates, and high-rises in Manhattan. When asked what he was going to do next, often he whimsically replied "I don't know. My credibility is shattered—would you buy a used car from me?" ■

6: BACK TO THE FUTURE

DID THE MOVIES
MAKE THE CAR, OR
DID THE CAR MAKE
THE MOVIES?

Nothing makes great, even legendary, cars into much desired and often valuable cultural icons than being cast into starring roles in successful major league films or television series: witness the Aston Martin DB5 used in a number of James Bond films; or the rumbling, grumbling Highland Green 1968 Ford Mustang GT 390 Fastback that flew high and crashed hard with Steve McQueen at the wheel in 1968's action thriller film, *Bullitt*; plus, the countless iterations of *Batmobiles*; and there are dozens more.

The DeLorean DMC-12's ticket to all-time film immortality was written by noted writer, producer, and director Robert Zemeckis, cocreator writer Bob Gale, production company owner Steven Spielberg, and a pair of whimsical characters named Doc Brown and Marty McFly. It all began in about 1980 when Gale and Zemeckis' most recent sci-fi collaborations basically tanked, and they were looking for some science fiction based on a meaningful, fun, interestingly nostalgic story, combining great acting, a brilliant score, and rocking soundtrack. They wanted something for the massive popular audiences that reached far beyond the interest levels of "geeks and nerds" and cooked up the basic tenets of what became the *Back to the Future (BTTF)* film franchise. Believe it or not, the studio pitch was rejected a reported 40 times before Universal would commit to a development deal, likely based on the strength promised by Zemeckis himself and the notion of Spielberg's Amblin Entertainment as the on the ground production company. Zemeckis had success and experience with rollicking adventure action comedies (such as the 1984 hit *Romancing the Stone*), and he and Gale would personally write and direct the production. Little did any of them guess that the ultimately three-picture franchise would become an all-time cult classic, big moneymaker, and a box office smash.

A handsome, charismatic, popular, young television actor named Michael J. Fox was the team's first choice to play protagonist Marty McFly, but Fox was initially written off as unavailable due to his commitments to weekly TV series *Family Ties*, so Eric Stoltz was signed to play the teenaged McFly.

Opposite: Given the powerhouse production, writing, and acting talent ensembled for *Back to the Future (BTTF)*, there was high expectation that the film would be good and good fun. Few could have predicted that it would become the cultural icon that it did, made Michael J. Fox an even bigger star, and had the legs in movie and pop culture history that it has demonstrated over the decades. *movies/Alamy Stock photo*

Even after several scenes and segments were already shot, Zemeckis didn't feel Stoltz had just "the right stuff" for who he saw as BTTF's curious energetic young teen lead. He was convinced Fox would have the perfect chemistry for the part and would meld with the balance of the cast, principally veteran actor Christopher Lloyd, playing "mad scientist" Emmett "Doc" Brown who was convinced he'd broken the code to time travel. The BTTF production team was so adamant about securing Fox for this film that they devised a seemingly impossible production schedule that would allow young Michael J. to meet his television contract obligations *and* star in *Back to the Future*.

In so many words, they would film *Back to the Future* at night, and Fox would continue his regular TV studio gig during the day. At the end of each day working on *Family Ties*, he would be collected by car and whisked off to wherever the Zemeckis set was working that day. He'd often take a nap in the car on the way over, get a quick shower, and roll right into makeup and costume for whatever BTTF action was taking place that night.

Back to the Future was to be filmed in and around California (in mythical Hill Valley) and on sets at Universal Studios, with principal photography beginning

Above: With Marty (Michael J. Fox) strapped into the time machine, he's now the hopeful time traveler that needs to get the car up to the critical 88 miles per hour (142 kph) just as the lighting strikes, sending enough power through the grappling hook extended from the roof up to a cable tied to the lighting rod to initiate the time travel back some three decades . . . and well, you know the rest. Talk about "timing is everything." *Cinematic/Alamy Stock photo*

Right: "Wait a minute, Doc—Are you telling me that you built a time machine . . . out of a DeLorean?" "The way I see it, if you're gonna build a time machine into a car, why not do it with some style?" Together, they're as famous an exchange of movie lines as ever laid down into film history. And fortunately, the first test of Doc's magnum opus invention to send his dog one minute into the future was a success, as both car and dog were safely returned when one minute passed by as "real time" caught up with the future. *Maximum Film/Alamy Stock photo.*

Below: As Doc Brown's DeLorean time machine streaks one minute into the future, it quite literally "burns out." The good doctor called time travel the "big one," the experiment he's worked on his entire life. *Maximum Film/Alamy Stock photo*

in November 1984 and concluded the following April 1985. In order to maximize the most active summer moviegoing habits, the release date was pulled forward to the July 4th weekend, 1985. The first *BTTF* film was wildly successful, racking up near record setting theater attendance and a strong reception from those organizations that present film awards. *BTTF* became such an immediate cult classic that it was followed by two sequels: *Back to the Future II* (1989) and *Back to the Future III* (1990).

The Stoltz-for-Fox lead actor swap wasn't the only major and costly plot substitution made by the writing and production teams. Doc's "Time Machine" was originally specified as a refrigerator, and according to writer and coproducer Gale, Zemeckis himself decided that the time machine needed to be a car and that the most appropriate car for that particular futuristic job was a DeLorean. This reputedly came at the behest of Spielberg, who vetoed any notion of people climbing into a junk refrigerator for time travel. His primary concern was that unwitting kids may choose to replicate these passages at home or in junkyards and become trapped and possibly accidentally die in locked defunct refrigerators.

Just hooking up a few lights and wires to a stock looking DeLorean DMC-12 would never do, so the car time machine was carefully designed and handbuilt, thus *cast and costumed* as would be an actual actor in any other leading role. Of critical importance was to get the look right, including enough techno whiz-bang looking hardware that it was believable not only as a movie-magical time travel machine, but also something built in Doc Brown's "mad scientists" lab. That meant lots of metal bits, things that beep and light up, all sorts of gauges and instruments, digital readouts and flashing lights, and the proverbial techno bells and whistles—the smoke and mirrors needed to sell the fantasy. Lawrence Paull designed it with artist Ron Cobb and illustrator Andrew Probert, all with legit movie making design cred. Ford reputedly offered a

Above: The über-authentically restored and functional *BTTF* "hero car" #1 DeLorean is still owned by Universal, but spends most of its time on display at the Petersen Automotive Museum in Los Angeles. It's a perennial crowd favorite and fits with the museum's mission to collect and display famous celebrity-owned vehicles and those that have famously appeared in television or movies. *Evan Klein photo*

Above: The *BTTF* DeLorean is more likely even more impressive from the back than it is from the front, as most of the exterior time travel stuff is bolted to the deck of the car. There's really still a PRV V-6 under there somewhere, but it's not likely the oil gets checked very often. *Evan Klein photo*

promotional fee of $75,000 and all the cars needed for the production to use a Ford Mustang as *BTTF*'s time travel machine, but that notion was kiboshed. Zemeckis wanted the exotic dazzle and futuristic appeal (stainless steel body, gullwing doors, etc.) of the DeLorean to sell the entire fantasy; a Mustang simply did not pack the desired pizzazz and therefore was not something Doc Brown and Marty McFly would have driven, according to Bob Gale.

The design team came up with a captivating yet somehow legit looking compendium of equipment, which was relatively easy to construct out of household, hardware store, computer shop, and military surplus components. The "Tachyon Pulse Generators," "Temporal Displacement System," "Particle Accelerator Canisters," and of course the all-important, now infamous, "Flux

Yes, there's a real, production DMC-12 underneath all the time travel techno wizardry here somewhere.

Capacitor" were all designed and created with these notions in mind. These "systems," how they are made, what they theoretically do, and what they look like in detail are covered in Haynes' *Back to the Future: DeLorean Time Machine: Doc Brown's Owner's Workshop Manual* (see Additional Reading and Resources). This recently published title, by coproducer and screenplay author Bob Gale and illustrator Joe Walser, is a wonderfully produced, lushly illustrated, detailed yet entirely whimsical glimpse at the look and technology behind the movie cars, stunts, and special effects. This DeLorean and *Back to the Future* fanatic must-have also covers the upgrades and evolution of the DMC-12 from its first generation look in the original film, plus its later configurations in the subsequent sequel films.

So just what is a gigawatt/jigowatt anyway? Wikipedia defines this mythical measure of electric power, and its relevance to the film as: "The power required is pronounced in the film as 'one point twenty-one *jigo*watts', with a jigowatt referring to 'one billion watts'. The spelling of jigowatts is used in the script and was also the spelling used in the closed captioning in earlier home video versions of the film. However, the correct spelling is '*giga*watts'. Although rarely used, the 'j' sound at the beginning of the SI prefix 'giga-' is an acceptable pronunciation. Later versions of closed captioning, such as in the 2020 DVD Trilogy release have corrected the spelling to gigawatts. In the DVD commentary for *Back to the Future*, Bob Gale states that he had thought it was pronounced this way because it was how a scientific adviser for the film pronounced it. The 'jigowatts' spelling is used by Alan Dean Foster in the novelizations of the second and third films."

Left: This is the VIN plate on the *BTTF* DeLorean. Even though it was produced in late 1981, it fell into a group of cars that ended up with "5000 series" VINs, despite the fact that 5000 cars had not yet been produced by DMC at the time. *Evan Klein photo*. **Opposite left:** The brilliant restoration work done by the DeLorean Time Machine Restoration Team really shines here, as everything lights up and appears in working order ready for the next take on set. Humorous analog touches include the decidedly un-high-tech cassette audio system, old school floating compass, and the dial pad that came straight out of a domestic push-button telephone. *Evan Klein photo*. **Opposite right:** Certainly, the most talked about, referred to, and quoted time travel component on the car is the now legendary Flux Capacitor. Don't forget to shield your eyes from its atomic light. *Evan Klein photo*

Wikipedia also does a credible job of describing the control of the DeLorean time machine thusly: "The control of the time machine is the same in all three films. The operator is seated inside the DeLorean (except the first time, when the remote control is used), and turns on the time circuits by turning a handle near the gear lever, activating a unit containing multiple fourteen- and seven-segment displays that show the destination (red), present (green), and last departed (yellow) dates and times. After entering a target date with the keypad inside the DeLorean, the operator accelerates the car to 88 miles per hour (mph) (142 kilometers per hour [km/h]), which activates the flux capacitor. As it accelerates, several coils around the body glow blue/white while a burst of light appears in front of it. Surrounded by an electric current similar to a

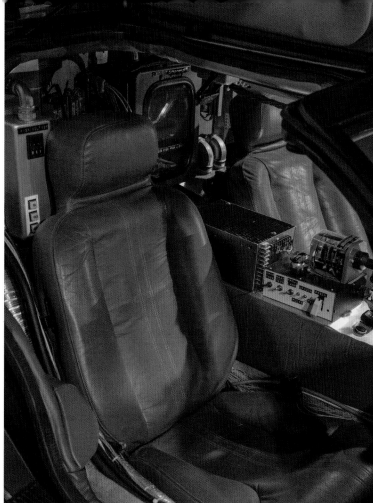

Tesla coil, the whole car vanishes in a flash of white/blue light seconds later, leaving a pair of fiery tire tracks. A digital speedometer is attached to the dashboard so that the operator can accurately gauge the car's speed."

All the legend, lore, and film history footnotes of these films and the cars can be traced back to the original version of *BTTF*. Doc's DeLorean was originally supposed to rely on atomic power to create the "fissures" needed to travel back and forth through time, yet it was decided that this notion was risky, impractical, and not believable (imagine that). This created a challenge and an opportunity for the script and the production team. It was ultimately decided that the requisite amount of gigawatts needed to effect the blast through time was obtainable through a precisely captured lightning strike, which begat the highlight scenes in the first film where young Marty needed to speed the car time machine up to exactly 88 miles per hour (142 kph) and contact a wire stretched from a lightning rod just as the lighting struck, providing enough power to ignite the time travel magic.

Left: The level of detail and dazzle of the original design and build, and of the restoration, is startling. It's no wonder these are some of film's most iconic movie star cars. *Evan Klein photo.* **Right:** Don't go looking for any armrests or cupholders on this center console. You literally won't "have time" to comfortably use either. *Evan Klein photo*

The detailing that went into converting a DeLorean into a time machine is nearly unimaginable, and of course everything had to light up, make noise, and/or appear to function.

Due to government requirements at the time, all cars legally sold in the United States were equipped with speedometers that read out no more than 85 miles per hour (142 kph), even if the car would technically go faster. So in order to sell the notion of a close-up action shot of the car on its way to the magical 88 miles per hour (142 kph), the design team needed to print a new readout for the speed, showing that its range extended to 95 miles per hour (153 kph). And a digital readout "speedometer" box was added to the top of the instrument pod to visually reinforce the notion of the car's climb to the critical speed.

And besides all the high-tech time travel gear, there were a few straightforward analog goodies bolted to the dashboard as well: An Airguide floating manual compass, a "Coustic" (as opposed to "Acoustic") AM/FM Cassette Radio, since the DeLorean's original radio location was displaced by other instruments and controls, a Bulova wind-up twin-chime alarm clock, and the aforementioned digital speedometer. For a deeper dive into every system, control, readout and technology involved in *Back to the Future* time travel, refer to the above noted Haynes Manual also referenced in Additional Reading and Resources.

Doc's DeLorean time machine remained architecturally similar to the original design, yet did evolve in order to facilitate the plots of the sequels. This included the car's on demand conversion to a hovercraft version of itself. SPOILER ALERT: One whimsical aspect of the DeLorean's conversion to a hovercraft includes a rear deck mounted device called the Mr. Fusion Home Energy Reactor that was in fact built for set out of a white plastic Krupps coffee grinder. Another evolution of the DeLorean was called the Off-Road Car, in which it wore steel wheels with chrome "baby moon" hubcaps wrapped by "wide whitewall" tires, plus of course, the version that needed to run smoothly on railroad tracks.

Right This car still wears its original low speed 80 miles per hour (129 kph) speedometer and apparently never got the revised applique sticker that raised the visual miles per hour limit well above the magical, much needed 88 miles per hour (142 kph). *Evan Klein photo*

How many cars were used for the filming of the three *BTTF* installments? According to writer and producer Bob Gale, for the original *BTTF* film, three stock DeLoreans were purchased, denoted as A, B, and C (cars). The A car was the most detailed and best-looking car. It was used for all the close-ups and beauty shots. The B car was less detailed and was used for wide angle and driving shots. On the rare occasion when both the first and second [filming] units needed to film with a car, the B car was always relegated to the second unit. The C car was used for interior and process shots. For *BTTF Parts II and III*, three more stock DeLoreans were acquired. Two of them were rebuilt as off-road vehicles, with more powerful engines and better suspension systems. The other was primarily used as the rail DeLorean seen in *Part III*, along with the A and B cars that also had train wheels installed. Additionally, a lightweight fiberglass replica was built for the wide-angle flying car shots in *Part II* that required the actors to be seen inside the vehicle while airborne. This was achieved by use of a forklift or by suspending the replica with aircraft wire from a crane.

As stated on bttfdelorean.com, "As of this writing, the meticulously restored A car [See Additional Reading and Resources for the information on this remarkable restoration] is on display at the Petersen Automotive Museum in Los Angeles, in fact, the car pictured at right. The B car was destroyed by the locomotive at the end of *Part III*, and portions of the C car were used to create a replica for the Universal Studios Japan theme park that was subsequently auctioned off to a Japanese company. One of the off-road *Part III* cars is in private hands; it has been beautifully restored and makes appearances at conventions and *BTTF* events. The rail DeLorean (along with the Time Train) was displayed at Universal's Florida Theme Park. Sadly, the fiberglass car deteriorated in storage and ultimately needed to be destroyed." Watch all three films and all this will make sense.

The moral of this story is that the original film cars are documented and well known, and if your neighbor claims to have found an original screen-used *BTTF* DeLorean in a barn or a shopping center parking lot, it's just not true. Replicas and *BTTF* "tribute" cars are relatively common within the *BTTF* and DeLorean owners' communities, and there are folks out there who will build you a very authentic looking *BTTF* copy DeLorean for around $40,000.

How did Doc's DeLorean behave as an actor on set? Ultimately, the cars did everything asked of them, or at least gave that appearance, but they were a bit of a handful to manage. According to bttfdelorean.com, "Second unit director Frank Marshal who had to deal with many of the DeLorean's action scenes recalled this in 1985, 'We were asking a car to do something it doesn't normally do. Unless you had hairdryers around you couldn't get the

Above: Sorry—gotta run. OUT A TIME. *Evan Klein photo.* **Opposite top:** Ancient Goodyear NCT radials must be as hard as carbon fiber all these decades later, certainly not safe or sound enough for 88 miles per hour (142 kph), much less time travel, but they complete the authentic look of the car perfectly. *Evan Klein photo.* **Opposite bottom:** The *BTTF* detail work is everywhere, even in some spaces that will only be seen fleetingly. Any idea how many plastic zip ties were used to bundle the car's many cable routings? Don't ask. We don't know either. *Evan Klein photo.*

Opposite top: The *BTTF* #1 DeLorean has been inducted into the National Historic Vehicle Register (NHVR) and spent time in this spectacular glass display case on show at the National Mall in Washington, D.C. The NHVR recognizes and includes vehicles of all stripes that are significant to automotive or other history, design, technology, and pop culture. The entire display, as seen here, was shown at the Amelia Island Concours d'Elegance in Florida and would have certainly won the People's Choice trophy had one been presented.

Opposite bottom: *BTTF* brothers, and still close friends, are lead actors Christopher Lloyd and Michael J. Fox, here at a recent Comic-Con event dedicated to the films. "The Future" wasn't as kind to Michael, who contracted Parkinson's Disease, but still lives a very full life with his family, having become one of the affliction's best known advocates in searching for a cure for Parkinson's. He no longer accepts honorariums for speaking engagements, with all those funds going directly into his Michael J. Fox Foundation. *Wikimedia photo.*

Above: The merchiverse is filled with *BTTF* memorabilia, including countless scale models and toys, not to mention myriad photos, posters, and clothes. Shop 'till you drop. *Kirk Gerbracht photo*

people out.' There was a constant crew working on the modified cars. Kevin Pike remembers how much attention the DeLoreans required to fulfill shooting requirements, 'It required constant maintenance. If it rained, it got wet, and water went down in the battery. There was no windshield in the back. You had to be able to take everything apart. You had to take all the vents off to even open up and get to the engine. You had to take the vents off to change the license plate. Transportation had to service it and change fuel and do everything they had to do to make sure it ran. There was a mechanic on set all the time that knew the engine inside and out, so they had their hands in it. There was a constant crew on that car from when the DeLoreans first came to when they wrapped the movie.'"

The screen-used movie car appearing in the photos herein is the actual, original A car, which postproduction parked outside in the Universal Studios Hollywood back lot and sadly left to seed. For a time, it could be seen by visitors taking the Universal Studios tram tour. It was damaged by weather exposure, and then *BTTF* souvenir hunters began to help themselves with whatever parts they could easily remove from the car. Bob Gale realized that this was the wrong way to treat an important piece of Universal Studios and indeed filmmaking and pop culture history and set out to see it restored and brought back to proper health and function.

To do the restoration right, Bob Gale made a potentially risky but ultimately historic choice. Instead of hiring a car company, restoration shop, or prop house to restore the car, Mr. Gale assembled a group of *Back to the Future* super fans to tackle the restoration. By doing so, the Time Machine became the biggest fan-led prop restoration in movie studio history. Joe Walser (Head of the Restoration) and his team of Time Machine experts had one singular goal and that was to restore the car with 100 percent accuracy, meaning every bolt, every detail, and every bulb and readout, exactly like it was in the movie, although more operational.

That kicked off an intense, year-long restoration. Grueling work and long hours pushed team members to their breaking point. Even so, their dedication never faltered. As Joe Walser often said, "our pain is temporary, but the car will be perfect forever."

The process was painstakingly documented by filmmaker Steve Concotelli and is available in DVD form, which can be purchased via backtothefuture. com or via Amazon.com. The production is appropriately named *OUTATIME*, honoring the license plate screen used on the car in the *BTTF* films. This documentary short film is very well made, extremely detailed and thorough, and includes interviews and factual materials from so many of the original team that was involved in creating the *BTTF* DeLoreans for the films.

And Now the Broadway Musical

Zemeckis and Gale have reputedly committed that there will be no further *BTTF* film productions beyond the original *BTTF, Part II,* and *Part III.* But that didn't prevent a group of nostalgic and creative musical stage producers from licensing the premise and engaging the film's original writers and producers to underpin the script and production values.

BackToTheFutureMusical.com describes it accordingly:

Great Scott! The multi-award winning Back to the Future The Musical is set to change musical theatre history.

When Marty McFly finds himself transported back to 1955 in a time machine built by the eccentric scientist Doc Brown, he accidentally changes the course of history. Now he's in a race against time to fix the present, escape the past and send himself...back to the future.

Experience this high-voltage comedy as the iconic story is adapted for the stage by the movie's creators Bob Gale (Back to the Future trilogy) and Robert Zemeckis (Forrest Gump) and is directed by the Tony Award-winning John Rando.

Back to the Future The Musical features original music by multi-Grammy winners Alan Silvestri (Avengers: Endgame) and Glen Ballard (Michael Jackson's Man in the Mirror), alongside hit songs from the movie including The Power of Love, Johnny B. Goode, Earth Angel, and Back in Time.

When BACK TO THE FUTURE THE MUSICAL hits 88mph, you're gonna see some serious...entertainment.

As of this writing, *Back to the Future The Musical* is playing in London and New York and also on tour around the United States. ∎

Above: It was bound to happen. Under the promise of no further *BTTF* film sequels, the basis of the first film has been redeveloped and recast as a Broadway-style musical, featuring all of the important original characters and a musical score comprising both film original and new showtunes. It's still enjoying an around the world tour as of this writing. *Patti McConville/Alamy Stock photo*

A DEDICATED AND
ENTHUSIASTIC
OWNERSHIP BODY,
PLUS A FERVENT
AFTERMARKET, HELPED
KEEP THE DELOREAN
FLAME ALIGHT.

mong the many travesties of the DeLorean Motor Company's demise is that we never got to fully see what the DMC-12 could become, evolve into, or spawn in terms of derivative models. John DeLorean and the greater DMC management and development team certainly had ideas for the car.

The complaint they certainly got the most, and most immediately tired of, is that the car lacked performance. Even in the somewhat performance starved early 1980s, 130 horsepower (96 kW) and 0–60 miles per hour (0 to 97 kph) in the 10 second range were not the stuff that exotic car dreams were made of. Even as carmakers were still coming to grips with how to crank respectable power output out of cars on unleaded fuels, while maintaining and meeting ever tightening emissions and fuel economy standards plus the need to thwart additional global oil shortage crises, turbocharging was already being turned to by both the automotive aftermarket and original equipment manufacturer (OEM) carbuilders as a means to juice up power and performance. Turbocharging wasn't anything particularly new, but it wasn't by any means as mainstream or common in the early 1980s as it is today.

Oldsmobile introduced a turbocharged V-8 engine in 1962, and the results were a bit underdeveloped. The turbo augmented aluminum 215 cubic inch (3.5 L) V-8 was not so coincidentally rated at 215 horsepower (158 kW). One horsepower (kW) per cu in (L) was quite respectable output for the day (made famous just a few years earlier by the fuel-injected 283 cu in [4.6 L] Chevy V-8 offered in the Corvette and full-sized models of 1957 and later) as was a maximum of 300 pounds feet (407 Newton meters [N·m]) of torque. Again, they're respectable numbers, offering performance also achievable by a variety of engines using less costly and more conventional performance methods than turbocharging. One of the Olds Turbo Rocket's performance foibles was a penchant for engine preignition, a.k.a. pinging or knocking. Olds addressed the problem by a separate tank that injected a water-based fluid into the induction stream that quelled the tendency to knock or ping. Ignition and engine management systems of the day were not sophisticated enough to sense the preignition and adjust the ignition curves accordingly on the fly to prevent the problem. In the end, it was all judged as too much hardware, cost, and hassle for too little performance gain, so the Jetfire's Turbo Rocket V-8 lasted only two model years, 1962 to 1963. The larger engine, higher

Opposite: Line 'em up! Much like Lamborghini Countach owners, when DeLorean clubbies gather, they invariably display their cars "doors up." Note the red painted DMC-12, fifth car from the front. *Dorset Media Service/Alamy Stock photo*

performance, better handling and more developed 4-4-2 muscle car filled its void beginning just a year later.

Chevrolet also famously offered a turbocharged Corvair that put out good power for its engine size and in fact cranked out more power than did a stock DMC-12. Although, by the time the turbo option was fully developed and began to really catch on in the marketplace, the Corvair's day was done.

The factory street car turbo scene remained quiet for some time, until Porsche, having learned what turbocharging could do for its race cars in the 1960s, brought a turbocharged production street model to bear in 1975/6. Called the 911 Turbo Carrera, or often referred to by its internal project designation, the 930, turbocharging cranked the 911's 3.0-liter (183.1 cu in) air-cooled flat-sixes power output up to a more scintillating 245 horsepower (180 kW) in a still relatively lightweight car. Something along those lines would truly put the DMC-12 in the proverbial pink. And being the guy who helped define

Below: The Oldsmobile Jetfire's styling was nothing particular to scream about but was handsome and sporty enough for the time—keeping in mind that the brilliant, primary colors and often overstated graphics of the late 1960s and early 1970s American muscle cars hadn't yet "become a thing." *Pictorial Press Ltd/Alamy Stock photo*

Opposite: You'll spot the turbocharger upper left of the engine bay boasting the Corvair Monza's 150 horsepower (110 kW) rating. Chevy beat Porsche to the air-cooled, turbocharged, flat-6 production engine by a bit more than a decade. *Marvin McAbee/Alamy Stock photo*

and crystalize the notion of the modern American muscle car with the original GTO of 1964, John DeLorean knew that's what his car needed.

So not long after the DeLorean's product and production specs were generally finalized, a gent named Fred Dellis, who operated a Porsche/Fiat dealership in Amityville, New York, launched an aftermarket turbocharging company called Windblown Systems. Windblown was offering aftermarket turbo kits for the Porsche 924 and front-engine, water-cooled Volkswagen models and was working with Fiat North America to develop a factory-offered Fiat 124 Spider Turbo. Dellis had made contact with John DeLorean, and the pair agreed they should meet to discuss the notion of a factory-offered DeLorean Turbo. It was about this time that Dellis changed the name of the company to Legend Industries and engaged the services of Chris Theodore, a successful product development engineer and program manager at Chrysler. He was immediately put in charge of the proposal for DeLorean. The turbo install that Dellis and Theodore cooked up for the DeLorean was not simply for a single turbo, but instead for a twin-turbo setup employing dual intercoolers for a cooler intake charge, which made for less ignition detonation risk and also more power. The pair met with DeLorean at his New York office on June 10, 1980. The discussion went well, all heads apparently nodding up and down,

as everyone agreed to proceed with a final equipment and pricing proposal and subsequent contract prior to parting company that very first day. Legend priced the twin-turbo kit, which was to be factory installed at DeLorean during production, at $3,888 per package, earning a firm order for 5,000 DeLorean Twin Turbo systems. He used Japanese IHI turbos as they were compact, light, "spooled up" quickly, and were cost effective. For Dellis' new company, and his new man, Chris Theodore, it looked like a walk off 19.5 million dollar home run, which hadn't event built out its engineering or production facilities yet. Early estimates indicated that the twin-turbo optioned DeLorean could crank out more like 175 horsepower (129 kW), a reasonable gain over the based, naturally aspirated V-6's 130 pony (96 kW) output.

Theodore visited Dunmurry to get measurements and develop a productionized bill of materials for the kit and its installation, and was dismayed to find factory buildings barely ready to produce a car. Once the facilities were equipped, staffed, up and running producing cars, Theodore was able to garner the measurements, drawings, and engineering specs he needed to fully

Today it seems that nearly every SUV has a turbocharged engine, but the notion was still somewhat rarefied (compressed) air in the '60s, '70s, and early 1980s.

Opposite: Bad Kitty. Porsche got ever more serious about street production 911 performance with the first "930" Turbo Carrera of 1975/6, recognizable and made ever more famous by its huge whale tail rear spoiler. **Above:** The Fiat 124 Spider still looks as great cruising the boulevards of Italy as it always did but could cruise them a lot quicker thanks to the factory offered turbocharged model codeveloped by the same company that worked on the DeLorean's. *Alex Friedel/ Alamy Stock photo*

flesh out the turbo program. The 175 horsepower (129 kW) number, as well as a 250 pounds feet (339 N·m) maximum torque output, were deemed feasible. However, the engineering teams opined that the PRV needed additional, and expensive, upgrades to be able to reliably withstand the extra boost load and higher power output. It was decided that "the ball had already moved too far down the court" to develop, produce, and deliver DeLorean turbos for 1981, so sights were set on 1982 production.

The system's development began in earnest in March of 1981, with two prototype DMC-12s and two of the similar engine Renault Alpines. Since the Alpines were regular production models and much more finished and developed than the two DeLorean hacks, Legend's first twin-turbo install took place on one of the Renaults. Theodore later commenting that "the lightweight Alpine was incredibly fast—0–60 in five seconds," a truly blistering performance for the day, handily outrunning most Lamborghinis, Ferraris, and Corvettes of the time.

Everyone at Legend knew that the PRV V-6 needed internal upgrading in order to meet ongoing performance and durability requirements, and

there was no provision in the previous contract to account for that or for who would foot those development expenses. The two companies agreed that the engine's shortcomings for this sort of performance application needed to be addressed at the factory level. The engine had a reputation for leaking oil into the intake valley between the cylinder banks and that its pistons, rings, and other parts weren't up to the higher compression stresses of forced induction. The engine's technical issues weren't such an issue in less stressed, naturally aspirated, lower power installations, such as the standard DMC-12, and the variety of more standard PVR models that employed the engine. Theodore prepared a presentation of the engine's inherent shortcomings and the fixes needed to address them at the factory production level and got surprisingly little backwash. It's likely that the PRV technical executives were somewhat aware of these issues and that its highly automated production facilities could accommodate the upgrades with relative ease, which of course would also improve the engine's longevity and useful life in all the brands and models in which it was installed.

One of the program's incremental highlights was a ride and drive exhibition test day at New York's Bridgehampton Raceway, where a variety of industry and investor types got to learn about the program in detail and side-

Above: The Renault Alpine A310 may have more in common with the DMC-12 than nearly any car other than the Lotus Esprit. Its size and general proportions are similar to the DeLorean's (sans stainless steel body panels and gullwing doors), and it runs a PRV V-6 engine out back. *Matthew Richardson/Alamy Stock photo.* **Opposite:** Fully DMC-dressed display model DMC-12 engine wearing the twin-turbocharged and dual intercooled turbo package that was under development when the lights went out in Dunmurry. *DMC photo*

A factory-offered twin turbo DeLorean wouldn't have cured every one of the DMC-12's engineering problems, but it would have fixed the one that most people complained about—the need for more power. Because of course "Absolute Power Corrupts— Absolutely!"

by-side sample a turbocharged example against a stock, naturally aspirated DMC-12. Everyone of course was impressed with the twin-turbo's tire melting performance, and in fact, the anticipated demand for the new high-performance DeLorean model was so strong that the companies agreed to up the initial order of 5,000 DeLorean Twin Turbo systems to 7,000.

No matter, by the fall of 1981, the skies were darkening for Legend Industries. Fiat was leaving the North American market, and other proposed turbo package business was thin on the ground. Furthermore, DeLorean sales had already begun to taper, especially as several American carmakers had elected to take their turbo development programs in-house. Legend limped through much of 1982 on crutches but with enough contract activity to keep the business afloat into 1982. Come the fall of 1982, you already know the rest of the DeLorean story. All of which put Legend out of business for good. According to Theodore, Legend Industries was DeLorean's second-largest creditor, having spent millions on engineering, tooling, and facilities for the DeLorean Turbo project. Legend never received a penny out of the DMC bankruptcy, closing the curtain on Legend Industries and the change for a factory offered high-performance, twin-turbocharged DeLorean DMC-12.

All That Glitters . . .

...Is, or could be, 24 karat gold plating. In its 1980 Christmas premium gifts holiday catalogue, American Express Corporation highlighted the cache and prestige inherent in its new American Express (Amex) Gold credit card by featuring countless, very spendy gold items within the catalogue's lofty pages, trumpeting that "The gold at the end of the rainbow is the most luxurious car in the world. The exclusive 24 karat goldplated De Lorean."

Such collaborative marketing initiatives between companies are often divined in the attempt to shed good light on all parties by associating their products, people, or services. American Express Corporation wanted something flashy for their annual holiday catalogue selection, and DMC always welcomed free advertising and PR, plus the association with a product carried by wealthy folks.

The plan was to produce up to 100 of these glittering gold DMC-12s. They were essentially, mechanically, and architecturally stock, save for a 9-micron thick layer of genuine solid gold plating on the stainless steel body panels and other assorted metal bits, such as the torsion bars that help lift up the doors and special dual exhaust tips. Anything that couldn't be gold-plated, such as the alloy wheels and plastic front and rear bumper fascia covers, would be painted to match.

In *John Z, The DeLorean & Me*, DMC Procurement chief Barrie Wills recounts the beginning of the story: "John Z was over in Dunmurry for one of his . . . visits when all seemed quiet, as everything at this stage, by our standards, seemed to be going reasonably smoothly. Everyone in the company was working flat out.

"The peace was broken when [company executives] George Broomfield, Mike Loasby and I were asked to join John Z in the boardroom. We arrived with hastily written crib sheets, from which we could update the chairman on our respective progress. John Z was at his most convivial when we opened the conference room door and filed in.

He went straight to the point and told us the American Express Christmas Mail Order Catalogue had the largest circulation of any [holiday catalogue] across the US. How interesting, I recall thinking. He went on to astonish us all by announcing he had finalized a deal for its front cover to feature a picture of a gold-plated DMC-12. That's good, we thought.

Then came the punchline '. . . and inside we'll be offering to sell 100 24 Karat gold-plated cars at $85,000 each to the first comers.' We stared at each other in disbelief. But this was for real. John Z was not joking—the deal was done." Now all the company had to do was design, source, develop, and produce them.

Unlike putting gold or gold-plated trim on design house concept cars, or single vehicles built for movies or television, batch producing a serial run of them, for retail sale, was at the time an entirely new undertaking. The DMC managers left their boardroom after their "gold-plated encounter" with John

Above: One of only two factory-built American Express Gold spec DMC-12s. This one is all original and virtually as new, with next to no miles (kilometers) on the clock. *Evan Klein photo.* **Opposite left:** DMC-12s never came with chrome or other exhaust tips. The factory pipe outlets were simply unpolished stainless steel neatly cut off and exiting just below the bumper on each side. The Amex specials, however, earned special accessory tips, fully gold-plated of course. *Evan Klein photo.* **Opposite right:** In the parlance of "gold trim packages" that showed up on luxury cars in the late 1980s and early 1990s, the gold-finished DMC grille badge didn't look so out of place. *Evan Klein photo*

Above: The "brown interior" Amex Gold DeLorean under construction in the special factory area set aside for the construction and security of these unusual and expensive machines. This one appears about done and ready for the catalogue. *Alexx Michael Archive photo*

DeLorean that day quietly hoping the whole thing would just go away. Unfortunately, it didn't. For better or worse, the demand for the car didn't equal or even approach the projection of 100 shiny gold Amex DeLoreans. In fact, the order total came in at two. Yes—two cars equaled the demand for them, and the DMC team needed to make them, and they needed to be running, drivable, fully realized, and otherwise production spec machines.

A pair of German chemical companies provided the formulaic knowhow and facilities and equipment needed to create such things. They were Degussa and Holders, both near Stuttgart, home to Porsche and Mercedes-Benz. A specially appointed team of factory operators were tasked with the physical job of turning two off-line production DMC-12s into gold-plated DeLoreans: one with a saddle-tan/brown leather interior and the other in black. The panels and bits were secretly trucked from Belfast to Germany for the dunking and polishing work. Once everything arrived back in Belfast, the assembly and fettling went on away from prying eyes in a special, penned off, security guarded

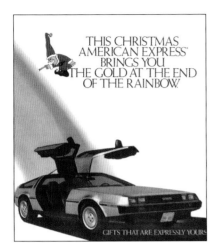

Above: Is it predictable or surprising that only two of these cars were ordered and sold through the Amex holiday catalog? Perhaps it was predictable in that what was originally a $30,000 or so car was priced another $50,000 more for gold that you couldn't wear or carry in your pocket. **Right:** Much reflected gold light really lights up the DMC-12 cabin. Notice the brown leather trim, beige carpeting, and automatic transmission. *Alexx Michael Archive photo*

area within one of the factory buildings. Both examples were equipped with automatic transmission, but otherwise appeared for all the world like standard, otherwise conventional DMC-12s.

In the odd event that a last minute order for an additional car was called for, or one of the cars was accidentally damaged, a third set of panels was also plated and prepared during the process. For better or worse, they were never needed for the furtherance of the Amex Gold program, and the golden bodywork went into inventory as spare parts. One of the door panels was somehow damaged along the trail and couldn't be properly repaired, so reputedly Consolidated International retrieved another stainless door from its own inventory and had it plated. The tonal match is said to be close if not exact.

The story goes that given the existence of these expensive gold panels in its inventory, Consolidated itself elected to convert one more car to Amex spec. It also appears to be an early car, although there is some VIN confusion about the whole affair. The car was faithfully converted to Amex spec and is equipped with an automatic transmission and a butterscotch/caramel leather interior. It is currently owned by Bill and Patrick Shea of Massachusetts, who have assembled a worthwhile collection of movie vehicles memorabilia, with a focus on *Back to the Future*.

It is noted that beyond the two cars converted to gold by DMC, and the post–DMC era example built up by Consolidated, a further few cars have been goldified by private hands.

Certainly not to everyone's taste, passion, or desire, the Amex DeLorean program and cars are a unique footnote in DMC's equally unique story.

It seems predictably early-80s tacky that someone would want an entire gold-plated automobile, yet it was an innovative idea, and certainly unique to this special edition DeLorean.

Opposite top: The wheels and wheel centers were painted. However, the lug nuts were fully gold-plated. (I wonder what the replacement cost per nut would be?) *Evan Klein photo.* **Opposite bottom:** Thankfully, all the gold action stayed outside the car. The company likely figured that the customer who would buy a gold-plated car wouldn't care too much about the engine. *Evan Klein photo*

Cottage Industry Aftermarket Dolls Up the DeLorean

It didn't take long for innovating, aspiring aftermarket companies to begin developing accessories and other bits for the DMC-12. A lot of the goodies that soon began showing up were relatively simple and straightforward to invent and produce—stripe kits and other graphics, mudflaps (really), dark gray plastic hoods or shields that made the headlights look glintier and more like single piece units, and chrome or polished metal lettering graphics that highlighted the embossed *DELOREAN* letters on the rear bumper. Then, some performance accessories began showing up, such as exhaust systems that with louder mufflers or that deleted the catalytic converters, all in search of a roomier exhaust note or much welcomed additional horsepower.

I recall being at a Ferrari concours one time looking at a row of red Ferraris, visually broken up by a bright yellow one parked in the middle. I made a comment about it to the guy I was with, that how interestingly the *Giallo Fly* (Fly Yellow) Ferrari popped out of a long row of red examples. He commented that "Ferraris are red, no matter what color they're painted." Much the same could also be said conceptually about DeLoreans, in that no matter what, they're *all* still stainless steel. The factory never produced any DeLorean with painted, colored finishes—all were built in the brushed stainless that so iconically identifies the car. The only footnote to that notion is to remind you that the front and rear bumper urethane covers were painted in silver/gray, in a shade that on purpose is not a perfect match to the stainless. This was done for several reasons: the first being that matching the look of brushed stainless in spray on paint was difficult if not borderline impossible and additionally, that the designers felt that those black trimmed bumper elements looked better if slightly contrasted to the raw steel. The shade was chosen to be complimentary and harmonious while still mating well with the steel panels, yet avoiding generally unachievable attempts at a perfect match. The look worked and remained throughout the DMC-12's production life.

No matter, it wasn't long before enterprising dealers, or car independent owners who wanted to make their cars "different from all the others," began painting them a variety of colors. According to James Espey's excellent *Buyer's Guide*, "three company cars were painted at the direction of DMC upon their arrival in the USA in May of 1981 . . . VIN 661 (red), VIN 667 (black), and VIN 672 (yellow)."

Properly prepping and painting the factory stainless steel panels required some extra effort and skill in order for the new paint to look smooth and properly bond with the metal in the name of longevity of the new finish. The car has to be sanded smooth, treated with chemicals, and properly primed before the new color can be added. The cars ended up in all manner of colors, yet looked particularly striking in black, which seems to accentuate the car's edges, lines, and black trim. Yellow and red are also popular. We've seen cars in various shades of blue and one in a greenish/blue teal that sounds odd but actually looks handsomely elegant in person.

Painting a DeLorean also creates a couple of circumstantial problems that prospective owners need to consider. One is that a painted car will always be worth less than one in well maintained, factory brushed stainless finish. Another is that it has been said that certain accident damaged cars were painted to cover up poorly straightened body panels. Stainless steel is virtually corrosionproof and generally robust material, but if over "worked" as might be the case in terms of straightening accident damages or removing dents, it can

Above: "Give an artist a canvas, and they'll paint on it." Such is the fervent imagination of the automotive aftermarket. The recessed *DE LOREAN* logotype lettering on the rear bumper was all the canvas some folks needed, as we've seen this space filled up with chrome or polished die-cut lettering and one such bumper sporting individually cut mirrored glass letters. Note the decidedly unfactory big bore exhaust system on this example. *Andrew Warburton/Alamy Stock photo*

Opposite: Each owner and enthusiast can decide if they like their DeLorean painted or factory brushed stainless. While to each their own tastewise, remember that a paint job could be hiding body damage, and that a DeLorean always loses some value when painted. *Dorset Media Service/ Alamy Stock photo*

become brittle, risking cracking in the future. And should an owner wish to return a painted car to its original factory looking stainless finish, it can be done, but it's a time-consuming and potentially expensive undertaking—so potential owners need to carefully evaluate how much or how badly they want a DMC-12 that's been painted and that if the look is to their liking or not.

A variety of aftermarket wheels have been bolted on to DeLoreans, and while some are attractive, it's important to get the wheel widths and sizing stagger just right in order to maintain the car's stance and handling. Given the car's wheel bolt pattern and sizing, most aftermarket wheels for the car need to be custom made modular pieces. One reason to consider this path is that it has become ever more difficult to source modern, high-performance, low profile tires for the DeLorean's original 14- to 15-inch (36 to 38 cm) diameter wheels (there are alternative offerings in the new tire market, although they won't be in the latest high-performance rubber compounds and tread patterns). So, those wanting racier low-profile 17- to 22-inch (43 to 53 cm) rubber will need to get wheels made accordingly.

It is amazing how many different engine and powertrain combinations have ended up under the rear decklid of DeLoreans. Many owners have gone the original factory inspired route of turbocharging the stock PRV V-6. Others "hot rod" the original engines in more conventional manners, such as with higher compression internals, cylinder head work, reprofiled camshafts, headers, exhaust systems, and such. These undertakings often yield varying results considering the owner's mission (and budget) plus the engine builder's skill and capabilities.

Small-block Chevrolet V-8 engine swaps are popular, as this venerable "bow-tie" V-8 is readily available from a supply standpoint, either from the proverbial "automotive recycling center" (junkyard) or even as new, fully as-sembled "crate engines" supplied by several aftermarket companies and GM. It takes a bit of work to make all the engine bay packaging fit (considering

that most engine swaps involve V-8s in a space originally intended for a V-6) plus transaxle adapters and such if the transmission is also changed. Needless to say, when engineered and installed properly, a V-8 engine of two to three times the power of the original V-6 does more than a little to brighten up the DeLorean's performance persona. Experienced DeLorean engine swappers also recommend using as many lightweight aluminum components as possible to minimize overall weight gains where the DeLorean doesn't need added pounds, meaning in the back end of the car. Many excellent high-performance engine offerings are available with all aluminum engine blocks, cylinder heads, and intake systems to minimize the impact of potential weight gains aft.

Interestingly enough, there is a "semi factory" engine swap that some owners have experimented with. The original PRV V-6 lived a long production life after the end of the DeLorean run and benefitted from many engineering and hardware updates along the way. Plus, it was factory developed and offered in sizes up to 3.0-liters (183.1 cu in), which naturally made more horsepower than the original 2.8's (170.9 cu in) 130 ponies (96 kW). Some owners have sought out used examples of the later 3.0-liter (183.1 cu in) PRV V-6 and successfully swapped them into DeLoreans. In stock form, the power gains are modest, although meaningful, and depending upon modifications to the exhaust and intake systems, can be increased above stock levels. For example, the 3.0-liter (183.1 cu in) PRV engine was installed new into the Dodge Monaco of 1990–1992 and was sold in North America, rated at 150 horsepower (110 kW). An engine swap to gain only 15 horsepower (11 kW) seems like a lot of effort and expense, although with somewhat upgraded internals as opposed to earlier, smaller versions of the engine may present a good foundation for further performance mods. It's also worth mentioning that if the DeLorean owner is only looking for modest performance gains, it's likely that given technological improvements in engine management and fuel injection technology, air intake systems, and exhaust systems, a reasonable amount of power increase can be gained from within the original architecture of the stock PRV 2.8 (170.9 cu in). By way of example, the European spec DeLorean, running essentially the same powertrain as the North American spec car, is rated at 163 horsepower (120 kW), a meaningful increase over the factory rated 130 (96 kW). The primary differences are the engine's state of tune and catalyst free exhaust. A 30 horsepower (22 kW) increase is something that will be felt in the seat of the pants and can be achieved without resorting to internal engine upgrades, turbos, or costly engine swaps.

Very recently, DeLorean electric vehicle (EV) conversions have begun popping up on the landscape, which depending upon your taste for EVs, isn't as far-fetched as it sounds. Depending on the electric motor(s) and batteries chosen for the conversion, the car will likely end up lighter than a stock DMC-12, advantageously taking weight out of the DeLorean where it does the most good—the aft end of the car. So, there are likely handling benefits to this approach as well. And given that electric motors produce their maximum torque at zero revolutions per minute (rpm), the performance should be stirring. Removing the fuel tank mounted in the central forward position in the chassis creates room for modern Tesla-style battery packs. One company, DeLorean Industries, produces a Ford Mustang Mach-E EV conversion package for the DMC-12.

Okay, an EV converted DMC-12 may not be as fun as plutonium and a Flux Capacitor, but this approach is modern, compelling, achievable, and whimsical in a *Back to the Future* kind of way.

Had it not been for companies like Classic DMC and an otherwise fervent automotive aftermarket, its likely much of the DeLorean story, and many of the cars, would have been long forgotten.

DE LOREAN MOTOR COMPANY

Classic DMC, Humble, Texas

Stephen Wynne was a mechanic by trade, and for a time in the early 1980s ran an independent auto repair shop in Los Angeles, which serviced DeLoreans, among other special cars. He was having difficulty sourcing parts for his clients' cars. In 1997, he put together a deal to buy the remaining parts supply from Consolidated International, which had acquired the leftover DeLorean cars inventory out of the bankruptcy just a few years prior and had no particular mechanism by which to retail or otherwise manage the parts cache or the parts business, along with certain naming rights and other intellectual properties associated with the previous car production. The new business was ultimately named the DeLorean Motor Company, and now in the potential light of a new organization planning to reinvent and reintroduce the brand and model lineup, is going by Classic DMC.

The original parts acquisition included many tons of OEM replacement and production parts, from new stainless steel body panels, to powertrains, piles of wheels, brakes, and steering parts, instrumentation, and lots of interior trim. Given this veritable fountain of youth supply inventory to keep DeLoreans young and on the road, the company also launched a restoration aspect to its business

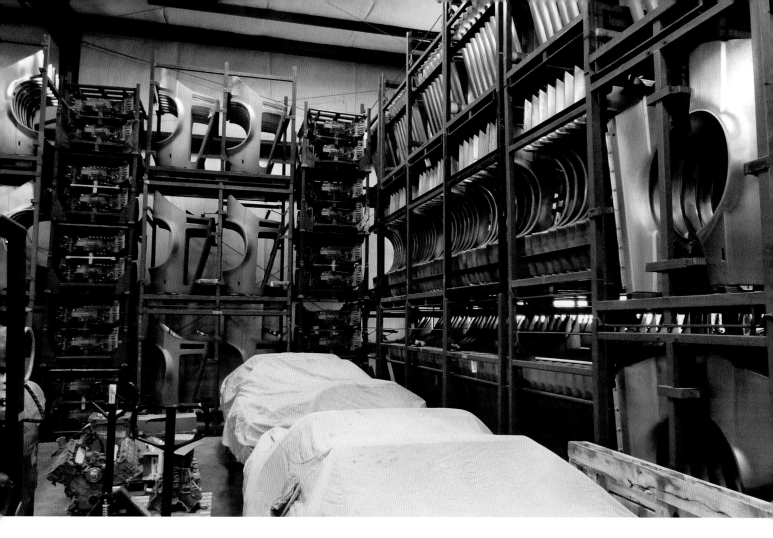

in the late 1980s. Classic DMC today stocks about 3.5 million parts over thousands of part numbers. In the case of certain parts for which no inventory exists, DMC has either sourced high-quality aftermarket substitutions or commissioned reproduction pieces to be tooled and produced. The company doesn't make a big part of its business in used parts but sometimes can fulfill that need if that's all that exists or meets the customer's need and request. In a few cases, new and reproduction parts are sourced from the companies that originally provided them to the factory in the early 1980s. The company also stocks full sets of shop, tech, and owner's manuals for those owners seeking those documents.

Walking through the company's 41,000 square foot (3,809 m2) facility, (nearly an acre under roof comprised of a 1,500 square foot [139 m2] showroom, 2,000 square foot [186 m2] offices/conference room, and 7,500 square foot [697 m2] service/restoration department capping the 30,000 square foot [2,787 m2] warehouse) gives a bit of a feel for what it might have felt like visiting the inventory buildings at DMC Belfast (or perhaps if DMC Dunmurry and Disneyland had a baby growing up in Texas). Everything is highly organized,

Above: Several of the warehouse aisles are filled with cars awaiting restoration. Lead times vary, but the waiting list to get your DMC-12 into the Classic DMC resto shop is about a year. **Opposite top:** Talk about *Real Steel*: fenders, quarter panels, doors, and nearly all the stainless body panels needed to completely restore a DeLorean, or virtually construct a new one, is contained within Classic DMC's operation. **Opposite bottom:** Vintage bins for vintage tin. Fortunately, in the long ago transportation chain from Dunmurry to Ohio to Texas, much of the original racking and storage devices for all of the original parts stores remained with the bits and are used in Classic DMC's massive warehouse.

racked, and numbered for location and inventory purposes. The company also produces some performance and other upgrade components, such as suspension and exhaust systems, plus handles nearly any service or maintenance items the car needs to make it right or keep it up to snuff. Besides the main facility in Texas, DMC has locations in Florida and California.

Every restoration candidate gets a partial disassembly and a full system by system assessment of what it will take to make nearly any DMC-12 as good or better than new, from the chassis up. Once Classic DMC and the car owner agree on a planned approach and a price, the car is stripped to its nubbins, and virtually every system is refurbished or replaced as required. The chassis is fully stripped, then repaired as/if needed, then rustproofed and refinished— or fully replaced with a new stainless steel frame. Then, the rest of the car is restored as specified and built back up in a manner not entirely unlike that of a new vehicle production process.

As demand (and the price levels) for fully restored, as-new DeLoreans increased, also born was an interest in having virtually new, built from virtual

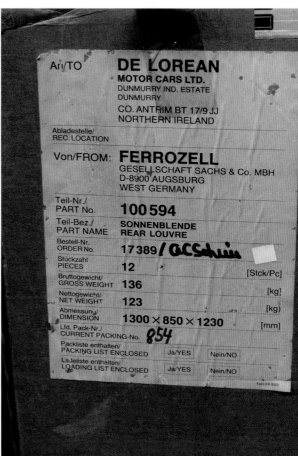

An/TO **DE LOREAN**
MOTOR CARS LTD.
DUNMURRY IND. ESTATE
DUNMURRY
CO. ANTRIM BT 17/9 JJ
NORTHERN IRELAND

Abladestelle/
REC. LOCATION

Von/FROM: **FERROZELL**
GESELLSCHAFT SACHS & Co. MBH
D-8900 AUGSBURG
WEST GERMANY

Teil-Nr./ PART No.	**100594**	
Teil-Bez./ PART NAME	**SONNENBLENDE** **REAR LOUVRE**	
Bestell-Nr. ORDER No.	**17389** / *OCSchin*	
Stückzahl PIECES	**12**	[Stck/Pc]
Bruttogewicht/ GROSS WEIGHT	**136**	[kg]
Nettogewicht/ NET WEIGHT	**123**	[kg]
Abmessun/ DIMENSION	**1300 × 850 × 1230**	[mm]
Lfd. Pack-Nr./ CURRENT PACKING-No.	**854**	
Packliste enthalten/ PACKING LIST ENCLOSED	Ja/YES	Nein/NO
Ladeliste enthalten/ LOADING LIST ENCLOSED	Ja/YES	Nein/NO

Top left: Books and manuals—they got them too at Classic DMC. **Top right:** Again, it's a wonder that so much original packaging and parts racking remains from Dunmurry after traveling so many years and miles to get to Classic DMC. Based on this label, it appears that the rear deck louvres were produced by Ferrozell in Germany and came a dozen to a case. **Bottom left:** Need brakes? Classic DMC got brakes, two by two by two. **Bottom right:** Classis DMC not only services and restores DeLorean's but also buys and sells them in a dealer or broker capacity. Sometimes, if an example is too badly accident damaged, it'll be stripped and sold for parts. That's Classic DMC president James Espey lurking in the background on the right of this shot.

Right: Classic DMC keeps a major stock of PRV engines (and parts) in all states—from worn out cores needing rebuilding, to partial engines often striped or sold for parts, to brand new, ready to install NOS V-6s. **Below:** The Classic DMC shop is clean, organized, functional, and always full.

scratch DMC-12s. Wynne and company devised a plan to set up its own mini, new DeLorean production line, made feasible by the huge warehouse full of new parts. The idea was to begin with a donor car, strip it down completely, and discard the original frame, replacing it with a new stainless steel back-bone chassis. Then, the car was to be built back up using a new engine and transmission, plus all new suspension. The fiberglass in the engine bay was to be substantially upgraded, as the original spec finish wasn't all so great. Then, the "new" car would be further assembled using new sheet metal, glass, doors, and door mechanisms. The plan included the offerings of a more powerful engine, sportier suspension, and a variety of interior trim levels. Substantially upgraded electrical systems were also part of the plan, which called initially for 25 cars starting at $57,500 in 2008.

Unfortunately, the project was stillborn, running afoul of emissions and other certification issues embodied in selling what is essentially a heavily restored 1981–1983 vehicle as a new car, no matter how new it was to be. No matter, the restoration business continues apace, offering much the same product as the "all new" plan would have, with a waiting list to get your car into the restoration queue. Classic DMC also handles the sales, acquisition, and brokerage of pre-owned DeLoreans. Or, if you need an oil filter, a wind-shield, a rear deck lid, or an engine, Classic DMC can still handle that too. For more information, visit Classic DMC and DeLorean Museum at classicdmc.com; telephone: 800/872-3621.

Left: Classic DMC's main shop area. The sign is an original dealer piece. Here's where DMC-12s come for anything from an oil change and a tune-up to a complete, from the tires up restoration. **Right:** A fully reconditioned DMC-12 backbone chassis, so far wearing its brake hose lines and fuel tank, on its way to a very factory-style buildup underpinning an in-process restoration. **Opposite top:** Here's an inter-esting look at the bits and nubbins of the instrument binnacle. The gauges themselves are very modular, but the circuit board is neatly printed, with very little wire chasing going on behind the scenes. **Opposite bottom:** More steel, more cars in line for restoration. Classic DMC's shop is very active, with cars shipped from all over to be made right or new again.

Top left: Classic DMC's showroom hosts the DeLorean Museum and is like Disneyland for DeLorean owners and fans. Lots of parts, photos, and other merch, plus things the company built, things they didn't build, and ideas they had but never got too. Just keep the drooling to a minimum please.

Top right: The rear sail panel window is installed with an industrial epoxy adhesive and uses these interesting screw down brackets to hold the window in place with no shifting or lifting while the glue cures.

Left: A beautifully restored DMC-12 and DeLorean chassis are front and center in the DeLorean Museum portion of the showroom, as they should be.

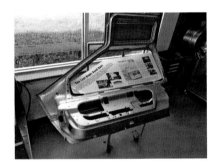

Above: The last and final right-hand DMC-12 door produced in Dunmurry is a story in and of itself. It's signed inside the door pocket by the team members that built it up, asking if it really was "the end of the dream" or not?

DeLorean Industries, Tallmadge, Ohio

DeLorean Industries stocks and produces a wide variety of service, replacement, and upgrade components and systems for the DMC-12, also ranging from stock, original style restorations, to a wide variety of restomod options and engine swaps they call the Reimagined Division. Upgrade options include "coil over" suspension systems, single and twin-turbo applications, full performance engine builds and swaps, transmission swaps and upgrades, and a considerable amount of stainless steel hardware. For more information, visit: deloreanindustries.com; Sales@deloreanindustries.com or Techsupport@deloreanindustries.com; telephone: 330/203-1018.

DeLorean Parts and Service Northwest

Located in Washington State, this independent shop and company supplies a wide variety of factory original and upgraded/performance parts. And if you're local to Issaquah, Washington, they'll work on your car too, be it a tune up, oil change, performance build, or restoration. They also stock and sell used parts. For more information, visit: delorean-parts.com; telephone: 360/358-3886.

Additionally, there are a number of independently hosted blogs, websites, and Facebook pages that address a variety of DeLorean service issues, modifications, and upgrades, as near as your closest Google search pages.

Opposite top: Not every corner gas station nor quick lube joint is stocked and equipped to service your DMC-12, so finding local qualified techs that can is rare and vital. This outfit, DeLorean Service Northwest, based in Redmond, Washington, appears to be up to the job. *DeLorean Service Northwest photo.* **Opposite bottom:** Just as proud DeLorean owners invariably park their cars "doors up," there's no reason not to drive in a parade in the same eye-catching manner, such as this gathering in Toronto. *NurPhoto SRL/Alamy Stock photo.* **Above:** DMC-12 *Splendor in the Grass* at this owners' club gathering in the United Kingdom. What appears to be gathering rain clouds in the background meant this was a decidedly "doors down" outing. *darryl gill/Alamy Stock photo*

DeLorean Club Scene

DeLorean owners club organizations have come and gone and also evolved over time and with the advent of the Internet and social media. As of this writing, there is no single, all-encompassing North American DeLorean owners club. One organization that presents itself as open to all owners and enthusiasts, regardless of locale, is the DeLorean Owners Association based in Norco, California: deloreanowners.org. There are several regionally located groups, however. Some exist primarily as an information exchange, while others host meetings and events. The DeLorean Owners Club UK appears to be an organized and very viable entity, with a vibrant website, publications, archive, clothing/merch, and show and travel events. In fact, this group has also staged pilgrimages to Belfast to visit the original DMC property and grounds in Dunmurry. For more information, visit: deloreans.co.uk.

There is also a variety of information websites, blogs, Facebook pages, and forums—fire up your favorite search engine and see what you find. You might also visit: delorendirectory.com. ∎

t never fails—gather with a few like-minded car friends around a DeLorean at a car show or parking lot and at least one of you will say "They should really bring back the DeLorean." Under the category of "Be Careful What You Wish For," it could just happen. A couple of new age DeLorean rebirth stories have been bubbling up as we write this, one connected to the Texas-based Classic DMC parts, restoration, sales, and service giant and another associated with John DeLorean's daughter Kathryn "Kat" DeLorean Seymour.

Prior to those explorations, it was beneficial to understand the future product plans that were boiling around DMC in New York and Belfast before it all went bust. In addition to the stillborn twin-turbocharged DMC-12 model developed and proposed, John DeLorean and his various teams were ideating a number of new products that could be produced in Dunmurry. Among them were giant mass transit buses and at least one four-door hatchback sedan variant that was rumored to be named the DMC-24.

Given the overall design success of the DMC-12, as well as both DeLorean and Lotus's excellent relationship with Italdesign, it was no surprise that DMC went back to the Turinese design leader to investigate its next models. The idea was imbuing a new, hatchback sedan with as much DeLorean design DNA as would look appropriate. It would have also been logical to incorporate other already done and paid for elements such as chassis and suspension design and components and the PRV V-6 powertrain too.

Opposite top: This non-running Italdesign DMC-24 scale model is rear-engined and looks credibly enough like a DeLorean product to remain true to the brand. In spite of the single door handle on this model, the DMC-12 would have worn two gull-wing doors per side—there's no mistaking those wheels. *Italdesign photo.* **Opposite bottom:** A DMC badge has made its way onto the driver's side taillight lens, and a lower rear undertray spoiler accompanies the winglet up on the rear decklid. *Italdesign photo*

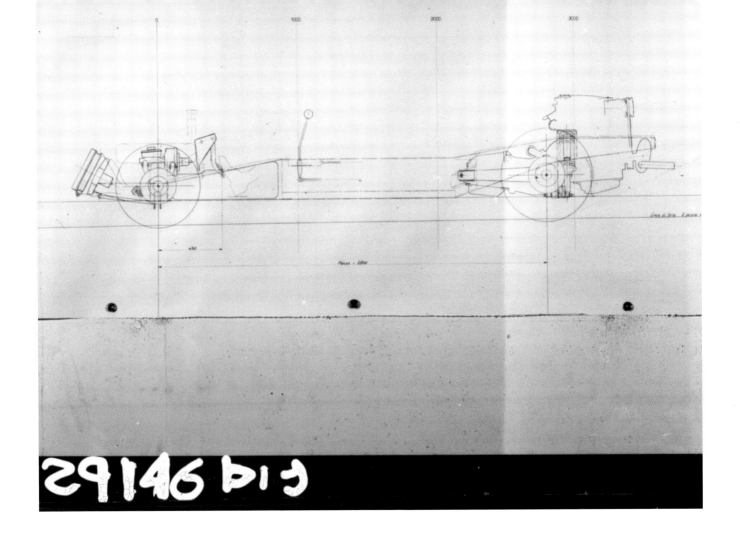

£14 04165

Opposite top: There's no denying that the DMC-24 would have been handsome and likely increased DMC's vehicle output and profit potential, but sadly, the car and the company never made it that far. *Italdesign photo.* **Opposite bottom:** Unlike the DMC-12, the mock-up for the sedan version was designed to have hideaway headlights. There's also a modest black rubber spoiler on the rear deck now, too. *Italdesign photo.* **Above:** This technical drawing shows us many things, including several of the car's critical dimensions and confirmation that the engine is rear-mounted as per DeLorean usual. The wheelbase is noted at 2,800 mm, or approximately 110 inches. Unfortunately, the markers for overall length are cut off in this photo. *Italdesign photo*

A chassis buck was developed incorporating a much revised cabin area to include a meaningful rear seat. Giugiaro and company developed a handsomely proportioned *quattroporte* (four-door) hatchback sedan that was designed around, not two, but four gullwing passenger doors. Many design drawings were done, and also one full-sized scale non-running model was built for auto show and prototyping purposes.

Sadly, the DMC-24 never, in DeLorean form, made it to the auto show and/or prototyping levels, as by the time the drawings and model were complete, bankruptcy was knocking on the doors at Dunmurry. This Italdesign concept was never officially shown as a DeLorean model, so there was no harm in repurposing the design for possible sale to another automaker. What could have or might have been but never was, the DMC-24 was restyled to become the Lamborghini Marco Polo design study. Lamborghini never picked up on the design nor developed it for production as a Lamborghini. It is at this point history's most significant fruitless DeLorean product plan.

ITAL DESIGN

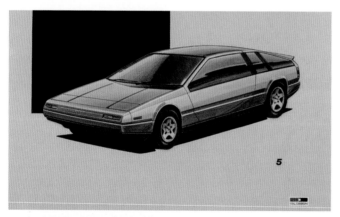

5

5

Above: Another four-door look DeLorean concept idea for a potential DMC-24. It's airy, glassy, and very European, but not as sporty as the look chosen that was under more serious consideration. Note the chunky four-spoke DMC wheel designs. *Italdesign photo.* **Left:** The rear look of the DMC 2+2 [our designation] shows a lot more glassline than does the original two-seater as might be expected. It is not believed that this design concept was seriously considered or mocked up or modeled full-scale. *Italdesign photo.* **Bottom:** A fascinating concept rendering, indicating that a 2+2 DeLorean model not having four doors was also under consideration. It's familiarly related to the DMC-12, but much changed and evolved from that car, too. *Italdesign photo*

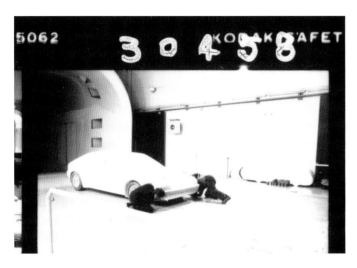

Above left: Aero models crafted of wood, foam, and clay tend to be very light, so they need to be tied down prior to sparking up a 100 miles per hour (161 kph) or more fan, or these techs could be also affixing instrumentation sensors to the bodywork. *Italdesign photo.* **Above right:** A DMC-24 model is rolled into Italdesign's wind tunnel for aero evaluation. Wind tunnel models at the time usually focused on the overall vehicle shapes, so it's common in this case that this model didn't have window cutouts, mirrors, antennas, or other trim bits. *Italdesign photo.* **Right:** The driver's side view of the same chassis buck shows the front suspension and accessory packaging, plus a hand cut, wood "headroom and roofline" marker showing how and where those bodylines could have fallen. *Italdesign photo*

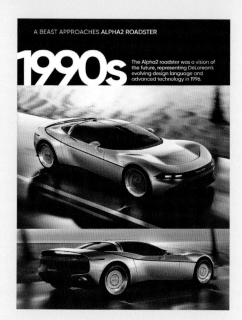

DeLorean Reimagined LLC

Imagine a conceptual sales and brand announcement advertorial brochure entitled "DeLorean. 40 Years Reimagined" that opens with "DELOREAN 40 YEARS OF HISTORY THAT NEVER HAPPENED."

Is it fantasy or revisionist history? Does it sound suspect? Many thought so. The company DeLorean Reimagined LLC, explained to journalist Aaron Gold:

Reborn and reimagined DeLorean creates a past to give itself a path toward the future.

Ask the DeLorean crew about their upcoming Alpha5 sports car, and they'll tell you it's the result of 40 years of ongoing evolution. But wait, didn't DeLorean go bankrupt in the mid-1980s? Of course it did—but the new DeLorean company . . . has created an alternate timeline where it didn't. Along with the Alpha5, DeLorean imagined a complete history of what might have been, including three seminal DeLorean concept cars.

We realize this sounds like an exercise in corporate navel-gazing, but when Troy Beetz, DeLorean's chief marketing officer, explained it to us, the logic made sense.

"We knew from the beginning that we couldn't just redo the DMC-12," Beetz said, referring to the original DeLorean production car. "The way we could make this brand legitimate was to suggest that the DMC-12 was a derivative of the DeLorean brand. And what is

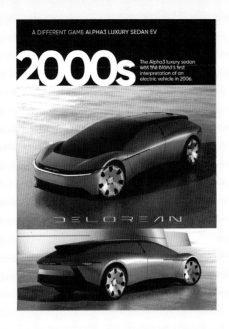

a DeLorean? What kind of company was it? We already had in mind what we were going to build, but there was no DNA to jump from the DMC-12 to the Alpha5. We had to reinvent the brand as if it were here for the last 40 years."

What DeLorean did was create a backstory—a fictional history of what could have happened in the 40 years since the DMC-12. The company did extensive research, looking at every auto show, every concept car, and pop culture trends of the 1990s, 2000s, and 2010s. "The work that went into creating the backstory was incredibly detailed," Beetz said.

Using the DeLorean DMC-24 concept . . . as a starting point, DeLorean worked with Italdesign to create concept cars for the aforementioned decades. Italdesign, as you may remember, penned the original DMC-12.

We asked, "What would DeLorean have done in those time periods to evolve the brand both design- and technology-wise?" Beetz said. "We weren't just exploring design language, but engineering and materials science, as well."

That's an awfully lot to unpack and somewhat recalls a not-so-popular political figure stating in 2017 that the then White House Press Secretary was speaking in "Alternative Facts." These three, theoretical, hypothetical, DeLorean vehicles (named 1996 Alpha2 Roadster Concept, 2006 Alpha3

Luxury Sedan EV, and 2013 Alpha4 SUV [sport utility vehicle]) illustrated in this brochure only exist in these lush photo illustrations. There are no scale models, prototypes, or moving, running cars attached to these glossy model names and illustrations—there are, however, Mattel Hot Wheels models. They all attempt to pave a footpath from the DMC-12 of 1981–1983 to the Alpha5 EV that the new DeLorean (often nicknamed New DMC) company is purporting to bring to market in 2024. Even though a couple of these vehicles are handsome and you may find their designs compelling, having come from the gifted minds and hands of Italdesign, they are conceptual flights of fantasy only and don't exist in any other medium. In reference to the 2024 DeLorean Alpha5, the DeLorean Reimagined LLC sales brochure states that "It is here that the real and imagined histories converge. If all goes to the plans made by DeLorean Reimagined LLC, the Alpha5 concept will become a real electric performance car you'll soon be able to buy." Is this, at any point, true and legit DeLorean history? We'd certainly be interested in John Z. DeLorean's point of view on this subject.

Even against the much more modern design of the Alpha5 concept, the original DMC-12 holds up well and still comes up as striking.

Opposite: Setting the brand stage and mindset—this is what you saw when you walked through the entrance to the DeLorean house in August of 2022, a perfectly restored, low-mile DMC-12 with manual transmission and gray interior. **Right:** Rocker panel logotype badging is a trick, clean, modern touch. **Opposite:** And just on the other side of the wall is the Alpha5. Some say it really recalls and looks like a DeLorean, while others disagree. No matter, it's an arresting looking car—let's see what it looks like in stainless steel.

Opposite top: Black rear deck louvers? Check. Gullwing doors? Check. PRV V-6 engine? Not check. New wheel designs and Michelin high-performance rubber are decidedly beefy looking—no Goodyear NCTs here. **Opposite bottom:** We're certain that this DeLorean house gathering in Monterey must have "broken the Internet" based on the number of Instagram and Facebook posts that went up during the event. **Above:** The Alpha's commodious passenger compartment, and it takes one rather humongous gullwing door to cover it. The look is airy, modern, and appropriately tech looking.

DeLorean Reimagined, which calls itself simply DeLorean, invested considerable money and fanfare in unveiling the Alpha5 to the public during August of 2022 on the Monterey Peninsula during the Monterey Car Week and Pebble Beach Concours d'Elegance festivities. The company rented a grand and expansive mansion proximate to Pebble Beach and decorated and staged it as the "DeLorean House." Various groups, individuals, and constituencies were invited for their chance to absorb the notions of the original DeLorean brand, the newly Reimagined brand story, and the Alpha5 concept machine.

The interior of the home was staged much like a museum gallery, with toy-sized car models of various DeLoreans displayed in glass display cases. Visitors could help themselves to "trading cards" of the Reimagined DeLorean History concepts. There was food and there were drinks—all intended to acquaint visitors with the brand lifestyle that DeLorean Reimagined hoped to establish.

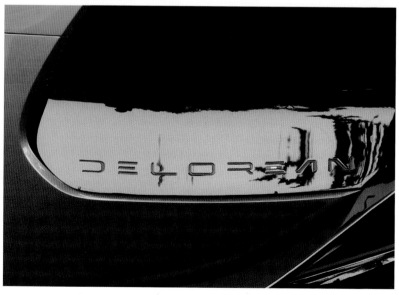

Opposite top: Alpha 5 development concept and old gold DMC-12 meet at the Petersen Automotive Museum, wing to wing. **Opposite bottom:** Several decades of style update evolution is clear in fresh, revised branding graphics on the "A5" concept. **Top:** The original DMC-12's sail panel and flying buttress designs hold up well, and don't at all look their age. **Bottom:** If anything dates the DMC-12 as an early '80s design, it's the quad rectangular sealed beam headlamp units. Still handsome, but clearly of a time. *Evan Klein photos*

Opposite top: We believe John DeLorean himself would be pleased with the look of the "New DMC" Plasmatail Shooting Brake concept. It encompasses seating for four, which is something he wanted to do, along with some meaningful cargo area without looking like a traditional, boxy, truck-based SUV. Note that the charging port flipper door is smoothly incorporated into the trailing edge of the driver's side front fender. **Opposite bottom:** Given the popularity of "Baja"- or "rally"-style production cars, it's no surprise that New DMC chose to investigate this edgy, out there, future design notion of an extreme off-roader in the Omega concept model, about or at least a decade and a half down the road. **Opposite:** Interior detailing of the Alpha5 concept models is modern and elegant, with neat red trimmed suede detailing, a front and center instrumentation screen, and adequate interior room in all dimensions.

The side entrance to the estate's massive patio, yard areas, and gardens first introduced visitors to a fabulously restored DMC-12, setting the tone for the branding exercise. Once past this DeLorean heritage display, again very much staged like a museum exhibit, guests entered a patio area fronting the home's garages complex. And there it was, glimmering beneath the spotlights: the new Alpha5 concept. Finished in an elegant metallic copper bronze color instead of the somewhat anticipated stainless steel skin, the Alpha5 pays certain design homage to the original DeLorean, primarily in its massive gull-wing doors, although the slatted rear deck/window treatment also recalls the original DMC-12. A pair of representatives from Italdesign were on hand from Italy to present the car to onlookers and explain its design philosophy and detailing. The car is very modern. It's a large two-door GT coupe with room inside for four, already a stark contrast to the DMC-12. Access to the elegantly trimmed cabin is via two long gullwing doors, not the possibly expected

Above: You can just about see the Corvette C-8's proportions and overall shapes in this DeLorean Next Generation (DNG) Motors purportedly under development by Kathryn DeLorean Seymour, John DeLorean's daughter. So far, the company has only offered renderings and now scale models or running prototypes as of yet. Stay tuned. *DNG photo*

four wings. The opening to the passenger compartment is much larger than expected, as are the doors. It's immediately clear and obvious that this vehicle represents an EV, based on the controls and instrumentation and the lack of a visible engine, exhaust pipes, and such. As you'd expect of a modern design study, concept car, or premium luxury GT, the extreme low profile rolling stock is huge, in this case on bespoke, center lock alloy wheels, their Blender blade design not in any way recalling that of the original DeLorean's Giugiaro designed wheels. Interestingly enough, there were no sales or product materials distributed, nor any speeches, informational, or welcoming remarks made by any company representatives.

Kathryn DeLorean worshiped her father, and is highly protective of his life and legacy. If anyone would try to back a DeLorean car company rebirth, it would likely be John Z's eldest daughter.

Once the Monterey Peninsula DeLorean House had been stripped and returned to its rightful owners, the DeLorean roadshow moved south to Los Angeles where the Alpha5 and two additional concept models were presented and on display to the public at the world famous Petersen Automotive Museum. The "2040 Omega" Concept full-scale plaster model was presented as an extreme dune buggy inspired off-roader set several decades into the future. It's an extremely avant-garde ideation of an extreme terrain vehicle (that might look very at home in a future *Back to the Future* film). There's no notion of practicality, or production reality, presented with this model but it does demonstrate the company is thinking beyond conventional on-road vehicles and also further into the future than 2024. Another more realistic and perhaps more compelling design concept, also presented in full life-size model form, was the Plasmatail SUV intended as a "shooting brake" extension or offshoot of the Alpha5. From the rear, the Plasmatail loosely recalls certain design language of the Aston Martin DBX707 hyper-performance SUV.

Go to DeLorean.com and you'll be taken to Reimagined's website that shows more detail about the car and the story, and explains a reservation and deposit system for those who are so inclined. As of this date, pricing, estimated production volumes, delivery dates, and distribution plan have yet to be announced in detail.

Thus, time will tell and so will we.

Next Generation DeLorean

John DeLorean's daughter Kathryn (Kat) DeLorean Seymour remains deeply entrenched in the greater DMC story and equally enamored with and defensive of her father. She has also hitched her name and interests into a vehicle, brand, and plan to bring the name DeLorean back to the new vehicle automotive landscape. She freely admits her father's foibles and missteps, yet equally feels he was an iconic innovator and that his legacy and accomplishments deserve recognition, remembrance, and rebirth. The most recent reincarnation of her plan involves a substantive rebody and remodel of the mid-engined, C8 generation Corvette, taking advantage of its well-developed mid-engined chassis and 495 horsepower (364 kW) all-aluminum V-8 powertrain. Eschewing the notion, thus far, of morphing DeLorean into that of an EV–based vehicle brand, the design sketches are compelling in that the car that's been ideated thus far is masculine, bold, and attractive. There has been some discussion about naming the new model JZD, honoring the initials of Kat's famous father. Plans proceed apace as of this writing. ∎

Was John DeLorean smart, or brilliant even? Without question. Did he make many mistakes along his life and career trails? Without question. But he was also thoughtful, contrite, and could also be apologetic and humble.

Post his two major trials, when we last left John DeLorean he was thrice divorced, again single, virtually broke, out of work per se, and living in a small modest apartment in the Northeast. In his autobiography, he described one of the paths to and through the drug trafficking trial in clear and harsh terms: "I was forced to liquidate my securities and real estate holdings at horrendous losses and a tremendous income tax penalty. Many of my other assets, such as car dealerships, my favorite cars, my real estate, and worst of all, my stock in the New York Yankees—had to go."

Still, by 1985, it appeared the worst of the ordeals was over—there were many outstanding legal issues and claims to be resolved, but the stress and deep troubles of the indictment, jail, and the trial, that appeared to engrave so much pain directly onto his distinctive face, were falling further behind him. His stress-driven health issues began to recede, and he looked again haler and heartier—once again, the proverbial silver fox. At the time of the trial, he was just 60, yet looked far more than his years.

Indefatigable, John DeLorean never gave up on his original dream. At the behest and insistence of his daughter Kathryn, he at first begrudgingly attended car shows and DeLorean car club meetings and was clearly pleased and surprised at the warm reception he received, signing countless autographs, signing DeLorean cars, and posing for just as many photos with car owners and fans. He spent many days and hours at his dining room table, working the phones to attempt to put another DeLorean car deal together. He commissioned renderings of an updated, presumably high-performance DeLorean, in red, boasting the large rear deck wings and bulging fender flares that had become so popular in the late 1980s and early '90s (think DMC-12 meets Lamborghini Countach LP500). You can find videos of him addressing DeLorean owners' groups, in one instance commenting that he is "working on the development of two new vehicles, both of which will have gullwing doors."

John DeLorean was often, and somewhat legitimately, tabbed as a high-flying guy with an equally high-flying ego. Yet, through age, time, experiences, inner reflection, and humility gained along the trail of his life, he became quite contrite as to his failures and foibles, particularly forthcoming and transparent in his 1985 biography.

Referencing a time in late 1981, when the company was up and running, and Dunmurry was rolling finished DMC-12s out of its loading dock, John stated that "what I did not know was that my determination to succeed would soon bring me face to face with men who shared my obsession for personal power and control, men who wanted to destroy me at any cost, for their own

glory. Nor did I realize that when I eventually looked into the face of the enemy, I would see my own reflection, for I too, had to triumph at any cost."

After his arrest and indictment, he admitted that "When one pressure disappeared, another pressure arose. And always I would ask 'why, me, God?' I never did anything to deserve such trauma. I never . . . But now for the first time, I really began to be open to answers. As I mediated about what had happened, I realized that I, John DeLorean, was a proud and arrogant phony. I had told myself that my objectives were noble. Everything I said sounded right, and made my motives seem pure and good, but deep down inside, I was really doing it all for myself. For John DeLorean. I was living a lie, an egomaniac, out of control."

It's one thing to have your dreams foiled, and it's another to have them trampled. Yet it's probably a third to see them tossed overboard out of a boat into the ocean. In 1985 he recounted, "We have recently learned that when it looked like DMC might come out of bankruptcy and rise from the ashes, the British government ordered the twelve million dollars' worth of body dies destroyed, dies essential for manufacturing the DeLorean motor car. Some of the dies were dumped into Galway Bay. Scuba divers have photographed the dies lying on the ocean floor. With this move, the British government destroyed the value of the . . . DMCs on the road to America." Several of the books about

the DeLorean company cars, saga, and man include these chilling photos, of the stamping dies aboard the deck of industrial looking cargo boats, prior to their reputed dumping into the brine. As with so many aspects of the DeLorean story, the net result of this action was unmitigated waste.

Over the years, and especially during my time researching this book, I've wondered and thought deeply as to why, where, and when, the whole DeLorean Thing went wrong. Did the entire undoing rest only and squarely on John DeLorean's shoulders? Was it the Reagan and Thatcher governments or GM, Ford, and Chrysler that conspired to put him down? Was it just not the right car, at not the right time? Classic DMC President, James Espey, whom we've mentioned several times, has had a front row seat to the entire DeLorean real life stage play for many years, so I asked his perspective. He said it was some combination of these notions and additionally that the company and the effort was "too thinly financed from the beginning, challenges of the transportation of cars and components all over the world to build and sell the DMC-12, negative reports about the car, and too much media noise about the bankruptcy and drug bust and all that. Plus, market recessions, hassles with the British government, and currency exchange issues that didn't favor such an international business concern." This is a straightforward, honest, and intelligent brief summary answer to the Big Question about Why.

Mr. DeLorean always spoke highly of his staff and the factory workers in Dunmurry and of the Irish People. He marveled at how such disparate men and women, deeply embroiled in political and religious conflict, could come together and work side by side, so hard toward a common goal—not only that of creating something great and wanting life in Belfast to be so much better, but for the burning need and desire to feed and clothe their families. He once said that "a lot of people questioned or criticized our plan to set up DMC in Belfast, but our problem there was never the people. I'm still happy we went there, and it's a decision I've never regretted."

You may wonder about the official address of the DeLorean property and factory in Belfast and what's become of the property since the bankruptcy and final shutdown. It's simple enough: DeLorean Motor Cars Ltd., Dunmurry Industrial Estate, Dunmurry, Co. Antrim. N. Ireland BT17 9JJ. The good news

Left: It would have been easy, and a huge waste, to let the beautiful DMC factory grounds in Dunmurry to simply go to seed or be vandalized into uselessness, and fortunately, that's not the case. It's also a certain brand of justice that the current occupants also produce automotive components. Here, a UK DeLorean owner's group makes one of many pilgrimages to the former home base property. *Damien Maguire Photography/Alamy Stock photo.* **Opposite:** Cheers, John. *Alexx Michael Archive photo*

is that the property and much of the original buildings and improvements not only survives (and thrives, in fact) but is still connected to the motor industry. Montupet, the French-owned car components manufacturer, took over the Dunmurry factory in 1989. The Dunmurry factory produces cylinder heads for the global car industry including GM, Ford, Peugeot, and Citroën.

John DeLorean remarried to fourth wife Sally Baldwin in 2002. He further settled down for quiet years with her in New Jersey. His realistic hopes of reigniting DMC and getting back into the car business were ostensibly finished, although likely never too far from his thoughts.

Like the late Dr. Martin Luther King, Jr., John DeLorean too had a dream (although granted of very different purposes and social magnitude). Both men touched their dream fleetingly, yet sadly never had the legitimate opportunity to see it fully mature.

John Zachary DeLorean passed away at Overlook Hospital in Summit, New Jersey, from a stroke, on March 19, 2005, at age 80. ■

Please allow me to again introduce Don Weberg. Don is a long-time friend and automotive journalist and publisher of note. Don's tastes in cars generally run to the fun, unusual, and eclectic. He has some interesting hardware in his small but meaningful automotive stable and of course, that includes a DeLorean DMC-12, something he pined after for decades. After several years since the original spate of DeLorean (man and cars) books were published, Don felt there was need for something new and fresh that focused strictly on the cars. John DeLorean was still alive and generally retired at the time, and of course, as any journalist would, he knew that his efforts needed to begin with an interview with The Man. He made contact, and it was an experience he won't forget and few DMC-12 owners and fans have ever enjoyed.
—MS

As a car guy from a car family, it's very possible that at seven-years-old a DeLorean was for me. It was at this age when I began collecting diecast toy cars from makers like Corgi, Dinky, and Bburago among others. My first was a red Rolls-Royce Corniche coupe by Corgi, which I still have today. Others filed in until I easily lost count, and yes, I still have most of them. This would also be the year that I would meet the DeLorean DMC-12 on a Buick dealership lot while we retrieved a new company car for my dad. The DeLorean was parked in the middle of the lot, between Buicks—it was so short and squat, it made the Buicks look positively tankish, but for me, it was perfect. Here was a car that was low enough I could see through the windows without needing my tippy toes. And that brushed steel that gleamed and glinted under the Los Angeles sun was unlike anything I'd ever seen. And then *those doors*. Good lord, the doors absolutely stunned me. I had to have one—at 7-years-old. From that moment on, the DeLorean was the car for me.

Fast forward to about 2003, and I decided it was time to write a book about the DMC-12. Finding a good book about the DMC-12 that didn't intermingle the drug fiasco and all the political gibberish was nonexistent. So, I thought I would write a book about the DMC-12 that would only discuss the car. My big idea also included having John DeLorean write the foreword for the book—so, I needed to contact him.

As an '80s kid, I had immense investigative training from *The Rockford Files*, *Magnum P.I.*, *Knight Rider*, and so on, so I set out on a quest to find

Opposite: The man, the legend, the writer, publisher, committed car guy, and the young rookie moto-journalist that located and interviewed the late, great, John DeLorean, with his own VIN 3900 DMC-12. And no, it's simply not for sale. *Caitlin Weberg photo*

Mr. D himself. It actually didn't take too long—a few phone calls to some places in New York, the last one being a church, and I had a lead on John's phone number. Remember, at this time, the Internet was still a bit of a wasteland, so it was all old-school tracking methods over the phone with 4-1-1 leading the way. Having gotten number after number from number after number, for all I knew, this latest number that supposedly went straight to John himself would be yet just another lead—so, I dialed and it rang a few times, when a commanding voice on the other end barked, "Hello?" This guy didn't sound like the other phone numbers—he made me a little nervous. So, I said, "Hello, my name is Don Weberg, I'm a writer in California calling for John DeLorean." The response chilled me—"This is he." Because I thought it would be just another number that would lead me to another number, I had no elevator speech prepared, I had nothing.

"John DeLorean, the car builder?" I blurted out as subtle as a train wreck.
"That's me," he said.

I'm not entirely sure what I blathered out at that moment, but I'm sure it was less than impressive, but John stayed on the phone, and we spoke at length about my upcoming book, his days at GM, his transition to launch his own car company, and a few personal tidbits. It was a friendly exchange, but it was definitely on his terms. His presence and voice exerted the command of The Boss. Or, maybe it was just a nervous 20-something-year-old talking to one of his heroes. He liked my idea of a book solely about the car and seemed humbled by the idea of writing the foreword for the book. He was interested in how I came across the DMC-12 and was really happy when I told him the story of the Buick lot; he brought up that he'd noticed a number of younger people interested in the car and attributed it to *Back to the Future*, which can't be argued—that film gave the DMC-12 the absolute forum from which to shine, a kind of second life without the drama from the first life. He discussed some of the dealings with Universal Studios allowing them to use the DMC-12 as the hero car and felt strongly that I should include a chapter about *Back to the Future*. "Felt strongly" translated to "you'll do this."

Through multiple conversations over the course of a few years, John supplied me with lots of information and edited the proofs I was coming up with. He offered oodles of advice and told me about various players in the building of the car, key players that made everything possible. While he never said anything bad directly about certain people, it was obvious he felt the company's success would have been better secured without their involvement. He discussed only briefly his family life at the time, and how difficult and strained things had become, but that in the end, he never lost track of how much he loved his two children and wife Cristina, who was famous in her own right. Finding out I was overweight and didn't exercise, he was encouraging, telling me about how health is a multifaceted sphere that included looking good and feeling good, with solid energy and robust strength. He reminded me that as he entered what should have been his retirement years, he started a car company, and he couldn't have done that without having kept his health in check. He also told me to wear good shoes, which I thought was entirely random, but it played right into his health mantra and made sense. Afterall, if your feet aren't feeling great, chances are, you don't either.

Through it all, I learned John had a few regrets, but overall, not many. He'd done what 99.9 percent of the automotive enthusiast and business population could only dream of doing—he'd run Pontiac and Chevrolet, and was on his way to running General Motors; he'd met and mingled and befriended some of the biggest names in the world; he'd dated and married some of the most beautiful women of the day; and he launched his own car company. He was what Hugh Hefner encouraged other men to aspire to become. Successful, charming, smart, daring—an essentially James Bond.

One day he called me and told me that he heard John Lamm's DeLorean book, *De Lorean: Stainless Steel Illusion* was slated for re-release. He said my concept was very similar, and wondered if it would be worth it for any publisher to compete with Lamm's already established and popular book. I wondered the same. I had Lamm's book and knew it well, and it would be very difficult to beat. I didn't realize it until that conversation, but indeed my book would have been very similar to Lamm's—just more hyper-focused on the car and the factory. Because of that, I suspended the project. Maybe I'd pick it up some time down the line. And now Matt Stone has done that.

John and I stayed in very light communication after those initial exchanges and then, one day, I woke up to find out he had passed away from a stroke. Honestly, I found myself glad for him. No more nonsense from any garbage stemming back to the car, bankruptcy, or whatever. He'd clocked out and left a legacy few could match. No regrets on my end—I got to spend time, even if only through phone, postal, email, and fax, with one of my heroes, and unlike so many others, he didn't let me down. He was frank and straight up, could be curt and maybe a little insulting at times—but he was nothing if not truthful with me about various topics, helpful when I thought I had an idea. I was sad when he died, he was one of the most brilliant minds the automotive industry, maybe the world, will ever know.

Fast forward to 2018, and I was finally able to acquire a DMC-12. It belonged to acquaintances who were retiring and couldn't take it with them to Florida. With just 20,000 miles, it had been through three owners and was in astonishingly original shape, right down to the original fuse box and fuses—if you know DeLoreans, you'll know why this is a big deal. Even the rear wheels retained the original Goodyear NCT tires, which needed to be switched out immediately. Working with a number of enthusiasts and professional mechanics, the car was brought back into driving status—fuel lines were replaced, the fuel tank was cleaned out, the master cylinder was rebuilt, the radiator and all the cooling hoses were replaced, the air conditioning system was refreshed, and, of course, Hankook Kinergy tires replaced the ancient NCTs and whatever was on the front. Many of these cars suffer from deferred maintenance—a lot of it. Fortunately, my car didn't suffer too badly, and we caught it early enough. I love driving my car, and it drives nicely, but there is still work to be done. Now owning one and hanging out with owners who work on their own cars, I've learned a lot about the factory deficiencies these cars were instilled with, but also that the DMC-12 underwent roughly 5,000 improvements through its production life, trying to make it a better car. A few owners I know drive their cars daily, one actually drives 200 miles [322 km] a day for his commute, and the DeLorean usually does this three or four days of the week, weather permitting—and it looks astonishingly clean. All of these cars do very well. Granted, owners had to work out a lot of the factory quirks, but fortunately there are a number of resources with parts and service to help not only keep them on the road but improve their performance.

I love my car, it's not for sale, and I fondly recall my interactions with John Z. DeLorean.

— Don Weberg ■

De Lorean: Stainless Steel Illusion
by John Lamm
978-0930880095

If you only plan to have one book in your DeLorean library (not recommended), this is likely it. The late great photojournalist and writer Lamm was there on the scene when it all happened, from John DeLorean's rise through GM, to his departure and founding of his own company, the development of the DMC-12, the birth and construction of the factory property in Belfast, the bankruptcy, and the early moments of John DeLorean's arrest on drug charges. This now out of print volume is credited as being particularly worthy in terms of the early days in Belfast and the development and prototyping of the DMC-12. It's not in any way a buyer's guide, but instead a worthy look at the man and a journalistic history of the pivotal events that shaped the DeLorean story—a must have.

John Z, the DeLorean and Me . . . tales from an insider
by Barrie Wills
978-0985657888

This is another absolutely seminal tome from DMC's longest standing employee and an important one at that. Even though his business card titled him as "Director – Supplies," he was the man who oversaw all purchasing of parts, services, and equipment for the company and the cars. Privy to many über-inside stories and truths and rumor about the man, the cars, the company, and the fall, Wills tells it all, straight and in meaningful terms. This book is also very richly illustrated with photos and documentation you're not likely to find elsewhere. Something else this book does better than any other is a meaningful acknowledgement and descriptor of so many hundreds of people who were also part of the story, at all levels. Technically out of print, although rumored to be in reproduction, you can find copies of this hard- and slip-covered book via

Amazon, some of the DeLorean parts and service providers, and the eponymous eBay. It's positively worth hunting down and having on your shelf.

Looking Inside: The Stainless Sensation
by Alexx Michael
PART NO. P100093

This book is subtitled A Scrapbook of the Most Incredible Story in Automotive History. And scrapbook is an appropriate definer. Running text, such as it is, is a bit choppy, but as promised, this book is laid out and organized very much scrapbook-style. You could research, snip, clip, snip, and Google for a lifetime and not assemble the depth and breadth of photos, illustrations, internal company memos, letters, note, advertisements, and other DeLorean materials and ephemera contained herein. A noted German rock and roll musician, songwriter, and producer, Michael freely admits that he's not a mechanic and instead, one who judges cars "by excitement, fun factory, and reliability." He became initially more directly familiar with the DeLorean when his pal Ace Frehley, lead guitarist for KISS, bought one in Connecticut and was subsequently involved in an accident, speeding, and car chase with police. Much of the information contained in this volume is utterly unique, and some of it you won't find anywhere else. It's currently in print and available from several sources online, plus Classic DMC and likely other DeLorean parts and service vendors.

DELOREAN
by John Z. DeLorean with Ted Schwartz
978-0310379409

This is John DeLorean's deeply personal and highly enlightening autobiography, published in 1985. It's a very poignant and personal voicing of his many successes and shortcomings, and only he himself could tell them. There's a lot of information on the trial itself, backed up with direct quoting from the official court transcripts, and lots of information to be learned about the car and the company, but even more about the man. It's out of print, but copies always seem to be around on eBay and via used booksellers and may even be at your local library.

DELOREAN Gold Portfolio 1977–1995
by R. M. Clarke
978-1855203310

This is another of Brooklands Books compendium publications of more than 40 period magazine and news stories about the man, company, and car. Rich with period road tests from most of the prominent car magazines of the day, these stories are packed with auto writer opinion, comparisons with competing models, weights, measurements, and performance test data. Strictly black and white other than the covers, this volume is super dense with the information you'll want about what the car was really like to drive and when rubbed up against the other cars that were its competition. It's yet another must have for fans and current and prospective DeLorean owners.

The Illustrated Buyer's Guide to DeLorean Automobiles
by James Espey, with Foreword by [former DMC chief engineer] the late William T. Collins, Jr.
978-0985657819

Don't even consider buying a DeLorean or even test driving one without having read every word of this pocket-sized book. All the production information, model evolution and iteration, foibles, and things to watch out for you'd want in a buyer's guide, from a guy who knows. His position as president of what is now referred to as Classic DMC, he knows every part on all variations of these cars and has shepherded the repair and restoration of many DMC-12s. There's lots of the usual VIN type info included here, and yet again, it's another must-have DeLorean publication.

Back to the Future: Deloran Time Machine: Doc Brown's Owner's Workshop Manual
by Bob Gale (Author), Joe Walser (Author, Illustrator)
978-683936216

Calling all *BTTF* fans—ever wonder the ins and outs of the DeLoreans used in the making of the famous *Back to the Future* trilogy? It's all contained in this delightful "shop manual." If you've ever wrenched on a car, you likely had a Haynes shop manual nearby. However, this book isn't exactly that, because it doesn't tell how to R(emove) and R(replace) the water pump, shocks, or brakes on a DeLorean (in classic shop manual fashion)—time machine or otherwise. Instead, it's a lavishly illustrated deep dive on how the movie car(s) were designed and built and about the people that designed and built them. Its humorously voiced and "narrated" by Doc Brown himself, and much of the text is whimsical and also goes a fair way toward explaining the science—real and imagined—at play in the time travel capabilities of Brown's "life's work" invention. Lots of great movie stills are contained herein, plus original drawings, concept renderings, and "design blueprints."

On a Clear Day You Can See General Motors: John Z. DeLorean's Look Inside the Automotive Giant
by J. Patrick Wright
978-028986963

John DeLorean's greatest successes, and some would say his biggest disappointments, came during his year at GM, both as a line engineer and divisional VPs at Pontiac and Chevrolet. He said he always felt a bit of an outsider there, punctuated by often tenuous relationships with GM's seniormost management and sometimes other managers within his own divisions. In this volume, he discusses a pervading "paralysis by analysis," confusing and often confounding product and design decisions made at many levels of the company. He also discusses his somewhat independent, maverick lifestyle and how that too often rubbed his bosses and some coworkers the wrong way. John later wrote that he wasn't completely pleased with every aspect of this book. It's still an eye-opening look at what was then the world's largest corporation. It's out of print but easy enough to find on eBay, Amazon, used booksellers, and quite likely your local library.

Framing John DeLorean
(documentary film)

This isn't a must read, yet instead a must watch. Over time, there have been a number of films and documentaries about the JZD story: some factual and well produced, some not so much. This one, starring Alec Baldwin in a highly credible portrayal of John DeLorean, works hard to portray the story as correctly as is feasible, without casting too much opinion either way. It chronicles "it was the best of times, and it was the worst of times" to paraphrase the opening line of Charles Dickens' A Tale of Two Cities. The production also includes a lot of recent, and very emotional, interview footage with Zachary and Kathryn DeLorean. The late Jerry Williamson, noted automotive designer, who worked for DeLorean managing the assets and production of many dealer meetings, and auto show appearances, said that of all the DeLorean films and documentaries, that this one is by far closest to the way it actually happened. It's available via most TV and video content streaming services.

OUTATIME: Saving the DeLorean Time Machine
DVD documentary

Ever wonder what happened to the primary DMC-12 that became Doc Brown's infamous time travel machine in the original Back to the Future? Believe it or not, it was retained—postproduction—by Universal Studios and left abandoned in an outdoor parking lot going to seed. Sun, weather, and vandals had their way with this historic movie machine, until it was clear the car would soon perish completely. The film's cocreator, and in fact the car's cocreator, writer, and designer Bob Gale, discovered what was (or wasn't happening) with the car and knew it had to be saved and properly restored. How and with whom this near heroic rescue mission came about is itself a somewhat legendary story, and it's all documented in this well produced video doc, available on Amazon or at backtothefuture.com.

The DeLorean Story: The Car, the People, the Scandal
by Nick Sutton
978-057333148

Nick Sutton was a longtime DMC employee, from near its barest beginnings, thus he'd been there, done that, and likely saw that. It's a bit "inside baseball," but if you want to study everything about DeLorean—man, car, and company—it's worth a read, although it gets into granular detail you will or won't entirely appreciate. The graphic presentation is nothing to shout about, but there are some photos contained in the latter pages of this compact paperback book that are highly compelling.

RadRides: Cars of the 80s & 90s as Art
by Geoff Ombao
978-1696746305

If you truly appreciate the design ethos of Radwood-era cars, you'll enjoy this artful book. It's also apropos that the DeLorean is not only covered therein, but also earns the cover art. There are varying graphic and design styles presented for a variety of 1980s and 1990s cars—and most will appreciate his personal taste in cars, including a DeLorean, a Honda S2000, and a Porsche 924S.

Old Men and DeLoreans
by Richard Smith
978-1365781599

A flight of pure fictional fantasy, this cheap and cheerful quick Amazon read is about a pair of adventurous old retirees bored with basking in the Palm Springs sun. A young man they know as a waiter at one of their favorite watering holes tells them about a cache (or hoard) of 50 brand new DeLorean cars, embalmed in a secret underground warehouse by his grandfather or some such older relative. Reputedly, the cars are perfectly preserved, and the intrepid trio elect to go a-hunting themselves for some DMC-12. Sure, like that's gonna happen. But if you want to be one that reads everything you can absorb about this mystical, magical, gullwinged machine, you might as well buzz through this too.

DMC Factory Workshop Manual
by De Lorean Motor Co. (Editor)
978-3941842595

Even if you don't own a DMC-12, or don't own one *yet*, you'll learn a lot about the car from this handy factory book, as well as a lot of useful information about how to maintain one. It's available from many of the DeLorean parts vendors, including Classic DMC, and also easy to find in PDF form for not a lot of money on eBay and other online sources. It's our last and final must have pub.

In DeLorean's Shadow: The Drug Trial of the Century by the Sole Surviving Defendant
by Stephen L. Arrington
978-0979957536

Mr. Arrington, among other things, was a drug running aircraft pilot for whatever cartel du jour would hire and pay him. He may or may not have been online to be part of the drug smuggling jobs had John DeLorean actually gone ahead with the FBI and James Hoffman's plans to ensnare him. Mr. Arrington seems more content here to share his exploits as a pilot, deep sea diver, and his female relationships. It doesn't have to be high on your list unless you really want it. ■

D

Dahlinger Pontiac-Cadillac, 25
Daly, Joe, 48
Dellis, Fred, 131
De Lorean: Stainless Steel Illusion (Lamm), 54–55, 79, 84, 182–183
DeLorean (DeLorean), 104
DeLorean Industries, 146, 155
DeLorean, John Zachary
    after scandals, 176–177
    arrest of, 100, 102
    at Chevrolet, 19, 23
    at General Motors, 6, 25–26, 28
    at Pontiac, 13–16, 19
    early life of, 10, 12
    fraud case and, 107–108
    GM Car and Truck Group and, 25
    personal relationships of, 6, 19, 20–22, 26, 28
    physical transformation of, 23
    pictured, *7, 11, 18, 20–22, 30, 69, 96, 105, 177*
    religious faith and, 103
    trial of, 103–104, 107
    vision for DeLorean and, 44, 46
    Weberg on, 180–183
DeLorean, Kathryn, 22, *105*, 158, 174, 176
DeLorean Manufacturing Company, 30
DeLorean Motor Cars, Ltd.
    Amex gold trim model, 136, 138–139
    bankruptcy filing and, 99–100
    comparisons with Esprit and, 82
    competitors for, 31
    DeLorean/De Lorean car name, 6
    dismantling of, 108, 111
    DMC-12, 9, 68, 72–74, 83
    DMC-24, 161, *162*
    Doris prototypes, 83
    dumping of dies and, 177–178
    Dunmurry factory facilities and, 32–33, 35–37, 50–54, 68, *71*, 84, *85–86*, 87–88, 178–179
    establishment of, 30
    financial troubles of, 94, 97–100
    first production DeLorean, 84, *86*
    leadership team and, 47–48
    marketing and, 60, *61*
    Pilot 9, 83
    prototype 2, 79
    public relations and, 48, 50
DeLorean Museum, 152
DeLorean Next Generation (DNG) Motors, 174
DeLorean Owners Association, 157
DeLorean Owners Club UK, 157
DeLorean Parts and Service Northwest, 155
DeLorean Quality Assurance Centers, 30, 84, 88
DeLorean Reimagined LLC, 164–166, 169, 173
    Alpha5, 164–166, 169, 173
    2040 Omega Concept, 174
DeLorean-Ryder Corporation, 25
DeLorean Twin Turbo systems, 132, 135
DeLorean, Zachary, 22
Dewey, Bob, 48

E

Elastic Reservoir Molding (ERM), 29, 63–65, 78
embezzlement claims, 30
engines, 56–58, 62–64, 68, 71–73, 79–80, 128, 130, 133–134, 143, 145–146
Espey, James, 89, 178
Estes, Pete, 13
"ethical sports car" concept, 29, 44, 46, 54–55